5th Class SUM Detective

Maths Activities for 5th Class

This book belongs to

Kilcolgan Educate Together N.S.

Please take good care of it and return it to the
school if you have borrowed it. Thank you.

FOLENS

Sum Detective is a series of maths activity books. It is in line with the Revised Primary Curriculum and has been written by four primary school teachers. Ample opportunities are provided throughout the series for both pair work and group work.

Sum Detective aims to provide students with mathematical experiences that are both challenging and enjoyable, thus making them more confident mathematicians.

Due to the variety of material included, Sum Detective can be used in a number of different ways:
- For the constant practice of maths facts
- As an easily accessible source of mental warm-ups
- To provide further revision of a concept
- As a useful homework book

Each book consists of 24 Units followed by a Dictionary and Mathematical Facts. Each Unit has 4 pages consisting of 11 sections: A, B, C, D, E, F, G, H, I, J and K.

Section A: Table Time provides constant practice of mathematical facts, helps develop and maintain speed of recall, and can ideally be used as a mental warm-up. In terms of a time frame the authors recommend allowing 3 minutes initially, then 2, and then 90 seconds. Naturally the teacher will be best placed to judge this allocation of time.

Section B: Try This introduces a mental strategy, and, having explained how it works, provides practice using it. This encourages pupils to search out patterns in mathematics and use them to help make computation easier. It also reminds pupils that there are different ways of approaching mathematical computation, some quicker and more easily executable than others.

Sections C, E, G and I: There are four mental mathematics sections in each Unit. While sections C, E and I cover all concept areas in the mathematics curriculum, section G is topic-related. If the topic has not yet been covered in the main maths class then this section could be revisited.

Section D: Vocabulary emphasises the importance of understanding the specific language associated with the Unit's topic. Mastering mathematical language is helped by the inclusion of a Dictionary section at the end of this book. A game can be played whereby the teacher calls out a term and elicits the correct definition or calls out a definition and elicits the correct term.

Sections F, K and J are mathematics puzzles and codes to crack. These challenge pupils to use their mathematical knowledge to figure things out.

Sections G and H will always be topic-related, involving a mixture of mental mathematics questions, and word problems.

The Teacher's Manual accompanying this series includes:
- All answers
- Assessment sheets
- A guide providing useful suggestions on how to make the best use of this series
- Further challenging activities including: Language Quizzes, Maths Puzzles and Brain Benders
- Photocopiable templates

Authors:	Kay Joyce Guinan and Yvonne Gleeson
Editor:	Sarah Deegan
Cover and Book Design:	Philip Ryan
Layout:	Denis Baker
Illustration:	Rachel Annie Bridgen, Emily Skinner and Sue Wollatt (GCI)
Cover Illustration:	Gary Blatchford, Mark McKenna

ISBN 978 1 84131 963 6
© Folens Publishers 2007
Hibernian Industrial Estate,
Greenhills Road, Tallaght, Dublin 24
Produced by Folens Publishers.

CONTENTS

A Table Time — Beat the clock.

1. 5 x 6 = ____
2. 8 x 7 = ____
3. 4 x 5 = ____
4. 3 x 4 = ____
5. 3 x 6 = ____
6. 9 x 7 = ____
7. 5 x 5 = ____

8. 8 x 6 = ____
9. 7 x 7 = ____
10. 8 x 5 = ____
11. 0 x 6 = ____
12. 4 x 7 = ____
13. 3 x 5 = ____
14. 2 x 7 = ____

15. 4 x 6 = ____
16. 3 x 7 = ____
17. 0 x 5 = ____
18. 8 x 4 = ____
19. 2 x 6 = ____
20. 5 x 7 = ____

/20

B Try this — Near doubles.

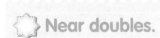 Near doubles.

13 + 14
13 + 13 + 1
26 + 1 = 27

1. 14 + 15 = ____
2. 11 + 12 = ____
3. 21 + 20 = ____
4. 42 + 43 = ____
5. 25 + 26 = ____

6. 30 + 31 = ____
7. 48 + 49 = ____
8. 51 + 52 = ____
9. 35 + 36 = ____
10. 29 + 30 = ____

/10

C Mental Maths — In your head.

1. 08:00 hours = 8 a.m. ☐ 8 p.m. ☐
2. 60 x 30 = ____
3. Which would you use to measure a mobile phone? Centimetre ☐ metre ☐
4. Write the number eight thousand two hundred. ____
5. Circle the larger fraction. $\frac{1}{9}$ $\frac{1}{8}$
6. Name this shape. ____
7. 84 ÷ 7 = ____
8. 480 + 220 = ____
9. 70 x 50 = ____
10. Circle the even number. 15 31 18

11. Which is better value, 8 sweets for 64c or 6 sweets for 60c? ____
12. Is this a regular octagon? ____
13. $\frac{1}{8}$ of 56 = ____
14. Write the Roman numeral for 5. ____
15. Is 3 a factor of 36? ____
16. Is $\frac{2}{9}$ bigger than $\frac{4}{8}$? ____
17. Circle the smaller number. 4044 4404
18. 6 ⟌ 96 = ____
19. A rhombus is a ____ pushed out of shape.
20. €9·50 + €3·25 + €5·00 = ____

/20

D Vocabulary

Wordsearch.

1. 10 years = one
   de_ _ _ _

2. To find the product of 2
   numbers we
   _ _ _ _ _ _ _ _ _.

3. 180° = a
   _ _ _ _ _ _ _ _ _ angle

4. 1000 ml = one
   _i_ _ _

5. 17 + 35 = fifty-_ _ _

6. A regular 6-sided shape
   is called a
   _e_ _ _ _ _.

7. 8 is a f_ _ _o_ of
   64, 32 and 16.

8. 4, 16 and 25 are all
   _q_ _ _ _ numbers.

9. 60 minutes = one
   _o_ _

10. Twelve = a _ _ _ze_.

d	t	h	e	x	a	g	o	n	u
t	e	l	q	l	l	i	t	r	e
a	h	c	j	t	e	c	g	d	g
e	x	g	a	r	w	k	l	l	r
f	y	x	a	d	c	o	y	z	o
h	o	u	r	n	e	z	o	d	t
v	q	n	u	n	p	l	a	n	c
s	y	l	p	i	t	l	u	m	a
x	y	j	k	s	j	z	h	b	f
q	s	t	r	a	i	g	h	t	n

E Mental Maths

In your head.

1. 16:00 hours = 4 a.m. ☐ 4 p.m. ☐

2. 30 x 80 = _____

3. 560 + 835 = _____

4. €10·50 + €1·25 + €3·70 = _____

5. Circle the smaller fraction. $\frac{3}{5}$ $\frac{7}{10}$

6. 8 x 8 = _____

7. 730 – 655 = _____

8. ∠ Is this a reflex or obtuse angle?
   Reflex ☐ Obtuse ☐

9. Round 6·2 to the nearest whole number. _____

10. Circle the tool you would use to measure
    the length of the school.
    trundle wheel   metre stick

11. ☐ Turn this shape 90° anticlockwise. _____

12. Name this triangle. △ _____

13. Is $7\frac{3}{8}$ closer to 7 or 8? _____

14. 0·3, 0·6, 0·9, _____

15. What is the value of 5 in 3852? _____

/15

F Puzzle

Problem of the week.

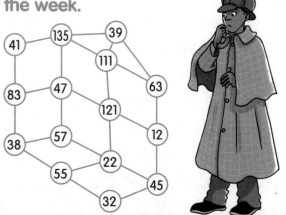

Start at 38. Do each sum. Colour the
correct path:

38 + 17 – 33 + 99 – 74 + 88 – 96

41 135 39
111
83 47 63
121
38 57 12
22
55 45
32

G Topic — Place Value. In your head.

1. Write four hundred and sixty one in figures. ____

2. What is the value of the underlined digit?
   53,684 ____

3. Write the number sixty-three thousand and three. ____

4. Write the number 2 before 2,000. ____

5. What is the value of the underlined digit?
   73,420 ____

6. The value of 6 in 7,462 is 6 thousand.
   True ☐ False ☐

7. Insert the correct sign: > or <.
   15,385 ____ 15,462

8. Write the number 30 greater than 4,038.
   ____

9. Write the number 50 less than 2,065. ____

10. Round 38,496 to the nearest hundred. ____

/10

H Topic — Place Value. Problem solving. In your copy.

1. Write the largest numbers you can make from these digits:
   (a) 4, 3, 9, 6, 1. ____   (b) 2, 3, 5, 9, 6. ____
   (c) 7, 6, 3, 1, 8. ____   (d) 8, 4, 7, 3, 0. ____

2. Write in order from smallest to greatest.
   (a) 33,641 33,582 33,976 33,104
   ____ ____ ____ ____
   (b) 58,631 57,453 57,989 57,966
   ____ ____ ____ ____
   (c) 73,465 37,465 73,645 45,637
   ____ ____ ____ ____
   (d) 11,502 11,052 11,025 11,205
   ____ ____ ____ ____

3. Continue these sequences:
   (a) 332, 334, 336, ____, ____, ____
   (b) 670, 690, 710, ____, ____, ____
   (c) 9,670, 9,680, 9,690, ____, ____, ____
   (d) 64,336, 64,436, 64,536, ____, ____, ____
   (e) 25,620, 26,620, 27,620, ____, ____, ____
   (f) 65,600, 64,500, 63,400, ____, ____, ____

4. Write the value of the underlined digits in words and figures:
   (a) 15,422 ____   (b) 43,250 ____
   (c) 19,306 ____   (d) 53,628 ____
   (e) 52,686 ____   (f) 72,636 ____

5. Round off:
   (a) to the nearest 10: 24,328 ____
   78,693 ____   32,497 ____
   (b) to the nearest 100: 83,350 ____
   63,794 ____   32,214 ____
   (c) to the nearest 1000: 36,445 ____
   48,500 ____   63,083 ____

6. Add 1000 to the following numbers:
   (a) 6,522 ____   (b) 28,465 ____
   (c) 39,420 ____   (d) 18,436 ____
   (e) 7,491 ____   (f) 450 ____

7. (a) Find the sum of 79, 19,302, 5,058 and 365. ____
   (b) Add 36,245 to the sum of 18,320 and 5,396. ____

/7

6

I. Mental Maths

Beat the clock.

1. (2 x 5) + 6 = ____
2. (8 x 3) + 8 = ____
3. (5 x 4) + 9 = ____
4. (9 x 2) + 3 = ____
5. (5 x 3) + 7 = ____
6. (6 x 2) +10 = ____
7. (7 x 3) + 4 = ____

8. (6 x 4) + 2 = ____
9. (5 x 2) + 5 = ____
10. (4 x 5) + 1 = ____
11. (3 x 5) + 10 = ____
12. (9 x 3) + 6 = ____
13. (8 x 2) + 3 = ____
14. (3 x 4) + 5 = ____

15. (7 x 2) + 8 = ____
16. (4 x 3) + 9 = ____
17. (5 x 4) + 2 = ____
18. (6 x 5) + 7 = ____
19. (2 x 3) + 4 = ____
20. (5 x 2) + 1 = ____

/20

J. Code Cracker

Each problem has a letter. Solve the problem and put the letter into the grid to reveal the message! You may use your calculator.

A = 16325 ÷ 25 = ____
E = 25 x 14 = ____
D = (256 ÷ 2) – 54 = ____

L = 87 x 9 = ____
S = 468 ÷ 18 = ____
W = 65,896 – 64,999 = ____

T = (8 x 2) x 16 = ____
H = 56 x 12 = ____
N = 876 ÷ 4 = ____

653	783	783	26

897	350	783	783

256	672	653	256

350	219	74	26

897	350	783	783

K. Puzzle

If your breakfast consists of 1 bread, 1 fruit and 1 drink, how many different breakfast menus could you have?

____

Bread	Fruit	Drink
Cereal	Orange	Orange Juice
Toast	Grapefruit	Milk
Scone		

A Table Time

Beat the clock.

Sherlock Holmes

1. 9 x 2 = _____
2. 7 x 3 = _____
3. 6 x 4 = _____
4. 8 x 5 = _____
5. 0 x 6 = _____
6. 5 x 3 = _____
7. 4 x 4 = _____

8. 2 x 2 = _____
9. 5 x 4 = _____
10. 3 x 6 = _____
11. 8 x 8 = _____
12. 3 x 7 = _____
13. 9 x 3 = _____
14. 6 x 5 = _____

15. 5 x 9 = _____
16. 10 x 3 = _____
17. 0 x 5 = _____
18. 3 x 5 = _____
19. 1 x 6 = _____
20. 10 x 5 = _____

/20

B Try this

Rounding.

Rounding

5 or more → round up

25 → 30

Less than 5 → round down

81 → 80

First estimate, then calculate correctly. 30 + 60 = 90 (estimate)

34 + 59 = 93 (answer)

1. 46 + 38 = _____ est _____ ans
2. 67 – 42 = _____ est _____ ans
3. 93 + 47 = _____ est _____ ans
4. 125 – 79 = _____ est _____ ans
5. 181 – 127 = _____ est _____ ans

6. 295 – 159 = _____ est _____ ans
7. 386 + 101 = _____ est _____ ans
8. 604 – 302 = _____ est _____ ans
9. 729 + 149 = _____ est _____ ans
10. 399 – 219 = _____ est _____ ans

/10

C Mental Maths

In your head.

1. 18:00 hours = 6 a.m. ☐ 6 p.m. ☐
2. 80 x 80 = _____
3. What instrument would you use to measure a garden? Ruler ☐ metre stick ☐
4. Write the number eighty two thousand four hundred and three. _____
5. Circle the larger fraction. $\frac{1}{9}$ $\frac{1}{19}$
6. ☐ Turn this shape 90° clockwise. _____
7. 6 $\overline{)108}$ = _____
8. 326 + 485 = _____
9. Which is better value: 8 apples for €1·44 or 6 apples for €1·20? _____

10. Is $6\frac{9}{10}$ closer to 6 or 7? _____
11. Circle the even number. 17 32 15
12. ∠ This is an obtuse angle ☐ acute angle ☐.
13. Find $\frac{5}{8}$ of 40. _____
14. Write the Roman numeral for 9. _____
15. List all the factors of 30. _____
16. 8 x 8 = _____
17. Circle the smaller number. 8,904 8,094
18. €8·50 + €2·00 + €4·50 = _____
19. What is the value of 6 in 38,641? _____
20. Write 15 minutes past 8 in digital form. _____

/20

D  Vocabulary — Wordsearch.

1. 2 lines that never meet are p_ _ _ _ _ _ _
2. Length x Width = _r_ _
3. A regular 5 sided shape. _ _ _ _ _ _ _ _
4. The outside of a _ _r_ _ _ is the circumference
5. 6 x 8 = forty-_ _ _ _ _
6. 0·1 = one _ _ _ _ _ (as a fraction)
7. A triangle with 2 sides the same length is an _ _ _ _ _ _ _ _ _ triangle.
8. A number that can be divided evenly only by 1 and itself is called a _ _ _ _ _ number.
9. A cube has 8 v_ _ _ _ _ _ _

a	n	o	g	a	t	n	e	p	q
g	e	i	g	h	t	w	r	l	a
j	i	s	o	s	c	e	l	e	s
h	d	v	v	y	d	j	r	l	d
s	s	z	i	q	t	a	l	l	b
g	e	a	i	x	a	e	e	a	s
v	e	r	t	i	c	e	s	r	r
j	h	t	n	e	t	f	o	a	l
f	e	l	c	r	i	c	u	p	f
f	g	n	n	e	m	i	r	p	h

E Mental Maths — In your head.

1. 22:00 hours = 10 a.m. ☐ 10 p.m. ☐
2. 500 + 700 + 800 = ____
3. Circle the larger number. 4,444 44,040
4. ⬡ Is this shape regular or irregular? ____
5. 1·1, 1, ____, 0·8, 0·7, 0·6
6. ∟ This angle is an acute angle ☐ a right angle ☐
7. 30% = $\frac{3}{10}$. True ☐ False ☐
8. 5 x 5 = ____
9. 0·8 is greater than 0·10. True ☐ False ☐
10. Name this shape. ____
11. 955 – 450 = ____
12. Circle the unit you would use to measure your classroom. cm m
13. €30·00 – €24·20 = ____
14. S. Is this letter symmetrical? ____
15. 46 ÷ 7 = ____ remainder ____

/15

F Puzzle — Problem of the week.

Each grid contains a path from every numbered square to the ■. The number in the numbered square tells you how many straight line segments it takes to get to the ■.

The paths to the ■ can only go horizontally and vertically and they cannot cross over each other.

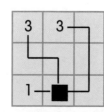

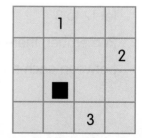

G Topic — Lines and Angles. In your head.

1. 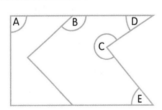 Is this angle a reflex or obtuse angle? Reflex angle ☐ obtuse angle ☐

2. 45° = acute angle ☐ obtuse angle ☐

3. Circle a full rotation. 360° 270° 180°

4. 89° = acute angle ☐ reflex angle ☐

5. How many degrees does the minute hand of a clock turn in one hour? ____

6. ____° = $\frac{1}{4}$ of a rotation

7. How many degrees does the minute hand of a clock turn in half an hour? ____

8. There are ____ degrees in every triangle.

9. X = ____ °

10. How many degrees in the shaded angle? ____ °

11. A straight angle = ____ °

12. Lines that go in the same direction but never meet are called ____ lines.

13. Name this angle. ____

14. An acute angle is less than ____ °.

15. An obtuse angle is greater than 90° and less than ____ °.

/15

H Topic — Lines and Angles. Problem solving. In your copy.

1. Find an example of acute, right, obtuse and reflex angles in this shape.

2. What 2 kinds of angle are made by the hands of the clock when it shows:

   (a) 6 o'clock ____   (b) 20 past 2 ____

   (c) 9 o'clock ____   (d) 5 to 5 ____

   (e) 11 o'clock ____

3. Through how many degrees does the minute hand of the clock move if it goes from

   (a) 3 to 6 ____ (b) 12 to 12 ____

   (c) 1 to 7 ____ (d) 9 to 6 ____

   (e) 12 to 3 ____

   Remember, there are 30° between each number.

4. Through how many degrees do you travel if you turn:

   (a) N to S (clockwise) ____

   (b) E to N (anticlockwise) ____

   (c) S to NE (anticlockwise) ____

   (d) SE to NW (clockwise) ____

   (e) W to S (clockwise) ____

5. Fill in the missing angles.

6. Fill in the missing angles.

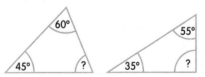

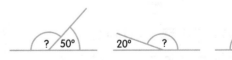

/6

Mental Maths

Beat the clock.

1. (7 x 4) + 4 = ____
2. (8 x 3) + 9 = ____
3. (9 x 2) + 12 = ____
4. (4 x 6) + 7 = ____
5. (5 x 5) + 8 = ____
6. (0 x 3) + 3 = ____
7. (1 x 6) + 8 = ____

8. (9 x 5) + 7 = ____
9. (4 x 3) + 11 = ____
10. (6 x 6) + 15 = ____
11. (0 x 7) + 9 = ____
12. (5 x 7) + 10 = ____
13. (2 x 4) + 8 = ____
14. (6 x 3) + 3 = ____

15. (9 x 3) + 11 = ____
16. (7 x 1) + 2 = ____
17. (8 x 4) + 6 = ____
18. (5 x 6) + 7 = ____
19. (4 x 2) + 4 = ____
20. (0 x 0) + 1 = ____

 /20

J Code Cracker

Each problem has a letter. Solve the problem and put the letter into the grid to reveal the message! You may use your calculator.

O = 2736 – 2043 = ____
E = 830 + 111 = ____
D = 638 + 113 + 25 = ____
U = (243 + 645) ÷ 8 = ____

S = 252672 ÷ 987 = ____
A = (821 – 65) ÷ 2 = ____
N = $\frac{3}{4}$ of 744 = ____
G = 3504 ÷ 4 = ____

T = (684 – 429) ÷ 5 = ____
R = 326 + 63 + 63 = ____
V = $\frac{7}{8}$ of 728 = ____
H = $\frac{1}{3}$ of (642 + 357) = ____

693	558	941

876	693	693	776

51	111	452	558

776	941	256	941	452	637	941	256

378	558	693	51	333	941	452

K Puzzle

Aidan fishes for a week. On a good day he catches 9 fish. On a bad day, he catches only 5 fish. On fair days he catches 7 fish. If he caught 53 fish in one week, how many of each kind of day did he have? ____

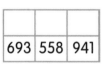

A Table Time — Beat the clock.

1. 2 x 3 = ____
2. 4 x 5 = ____
3. 7 x 2 = ____
4. 9 x 4 = ____
5. 6 x 3 = ____
6. 5 x 4 = ____
7. 9 x 5 = ____

8. 3 x 3 = ____
9. 6 x 5 = ____
10. 4 x 2 = ____
11. 8 x 4 = ____
12. 5 x 3 = ____
13. 6 x 4 = ____
14. 8 x 2 = ____

15. 4 x 3 = ____
16. 7 x 5 = ____
17. 9 x 2 = ____
18. 7 x 4 = ____
19. 9 x 3 = ____
20. 4 x 4 = ____

/20

B Try this — Near doubles.

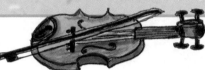

Near doubles

12 + 14

12 + 12 + 2

24 + 2 = 26

1. 15 + 16 = ____
2. 20 + 19 = ____
3. 14 + 13 = ____
4. 33 + 32 = ____
5. 25 + 24 = ____
6. 19 + 20 = ____
7. 36 + 37 = ____
8. 25 + 26 = ____

9. 90 + 91 = ____
10. 69 + 70 = ____
11. 8 + 9 = ____
12. 10 + 11 = ____
13. 14 + 15 = ____
14. 29 + 30 = ____
15. 50 + 49 = ____

/15

C Mental Maths — In your head.

1. 03:00 hours = 3 a.m. ☐ 3 p.m. ☐
2. 50 x 40 = ____
3. Which would you use to measure your copy? cm ☐ m ☐
4. Write the number ten thousand. ____
5. Circle the larger fraction. $\frac{1}{4}$ $\frac{1}{8}$
6. 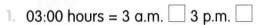 Name this 3D shape. ____
7. 90 ÷ 5 = ____
8. 250 + 650 = ____
9. 20 x 60 = ____
10. Circle the even number. 3 6 9

11. Which is better value, 5 apples for 75c or 4 apples for 48c? ____
12. Is this a regular or an irregular pentagon? ____
13. $\frac{1}{3}$ of 15 = ____
14. Write the Roman numeral for 4. ____
15. Is 4 a factor of 28? ____
16. Is $\frac{1}{2}$ bigger than $\frac{1}{3}$? ____
17. Circle the smaller number. 10,010 10,001
18. 5 ⟌ 70 = ____
19. Are all the angles equal in a square? ____
20. €4·00 + €2·25 + €1·50 = ____

/20

D Vocabulary

Wordsearch.

1. 100 years = one
   c_ _ _ _ _ _ _

2. 14 days = one
   _ _ _ _ _ _ _ _ t

3. 1000 mm = one
   _ _ _ _ _

4. 12 months = one
   _ _ _ _

5. 5 is the a_ _ _ _ _ _ _
   of 6, 8 and 1.

6. To find the difference
   between 2 numbers, we
   s_ _ _ _ _ _ _.

7. Corner of 3D shapes =
   a _ _ _t_ _

8. Always do what is in the
   _r_ _ _ _ _ _ first.

9. A regular 5-sided shape
   = a _ _ _ _ g_ _

10. 90° = a _ _ _ _ _
    angle.

p	s	t	e	k	c	a	r̄	b	k
e	r	y	x	v	e	r	t	e	x
n	n	i	e	s	n	a	e	m	r
t	z	q	g	a	a	y	t	h	p
a	e	o	w	h	r	t	a	f	y
g	r	k	h	r	t	f	h	i	v
o	t	h	g	i	n	t	r	o	f
n	e	g	a	r	e	v	a	g	z
g	m	t	c	a	r	t	b	u	s
t	y	r	u	t	n	e	c	y	m

E Mental Maths

In your head.

1. 14:00 hours = 2 a.m. ☐ 2 p.m. ☐
2. 90 x 60 = ____
3. Circle the tool you would use to measure a door. ruler   metre stick
4. Write the number twenty two thousand and eleven. ____
5. Circle the larger fraction. $\frac{1}{4}$ $\frac{3}{8}$
6. Turn this shape 90° clockwise. ☐⊢ ____
7. $4 \overline{)96}$ = ____
8. 975 + 350 = ____
9. Is $5\frac{3}{10}$ closer to 5 or 6? ____
10. Circle the odd numbers. 16 19 22

11. Which is better value, 9 bananas for 90c or 4 bananas for 60c?
12. ⟋ Is this angle an acute or reflex angle? Acute angle ☐ reflex angle ☐
13. $\frac{3}{4}$ of 32 = ____
14. ▱ Name this 3D shape. ____
15. List all the factors of 20. ____
16. 6 x 6 = ____
17. Circle the smaller number. 40,402 44,020
18. What is the value of 3 in 58,365? ____
19. Write 20 past 5 in digital form. ____
20. €2·05 + €4·20 + €3·50 = ____

/20

F Puzzle

Problem of the week.

Fill in the digits 1 to 9 to make 2 different ways to get the sum 1,000. You can only use each digit once in each sum.

____ ____ ____ + ____ ____ ____ = 1,000   ____ ____ ____ + ____ ____ ____ = 1,000

G. Topic — Averages. In your head.

1. Find the average of 7, 9 and 11. ____
2. Find the average of 40 min, 20 min, 55 min, 45 min and 35 min. ____
3. Find the average of 9, 11 and 13. ____
4. John is 11. His brother is 4 years younger. What is their average age? ____
5. Find the average of 12, 22 and 17. ____
6. Find the average of 26, 36, 46, 56 and 66. ____
7. Find the average of 6, 8 and 10. ____
8. The average of 4 numbers is 15. What is their total? ____

9. Find the average of 4, 11 and 12. ____
10. The average of 3 numbers is 8. Two of the numbers are 11 and 6. What is the 3rd? ____
11. Find the average of 7, 9 and 14. ____
12. The average cost of 7 books is €8·30. What is the total cost? ____
13. Find the average of 3, 5, 7 and 9. ____
14. Three balls cost €11·00, €9·50 and €12·50 each. What is the average price? ____
15. Find the average of 6, 12 and 18. ____

/15

H. Topic — Averages. Problem solving. In your copy.

1. Tom, Mary, Aoife, Ronan and Jer are aged 8, 9, 11, 10 and 7. What is their average age? ____
2. 4 children get different amounts of pocket money. They are 40c, 80c, 70c and 50c. What is the average pocket money? ____
3. Find the average of:
   (a) €27, €55 and €44. ____
   (b) 22 cm, 49 cm and 64 cm. ____
   (c) 33 kg, 43 kg, 59 kg and 61 kg. ____
4. Find the average price of three footballs that cost €5·60, €9·40 and €11·22 each. ____
5. John cycled 25 km, 15 km, 21 km and 19 km over 4 days. How far on average did he travel each day? ____
6. The average cost of a pair of jeans is €53·45. Find the cost of 6 pairs. ____

7.

	Height	Weight
Tom	1·08 m	31·46 kg
Mary	1·51 m	27·30 kg
Brian	1·36 m	34·38 kg
Ciaran	1·29 m	27·30 kg

(a) What is the average height? ____
(b) What is the average weight? ____
(c) How many children are above the average height? ____
(d) How many children are below the average weight? ____

8. A teacher bought 7 library books at an average price of €10·21 and 3 art books at an average price of €5·99. What was the total bill? ____

/8

Mental Maths

Beat the clock.

1. What time is it now? _____
2. 29 + 35 = _____
3. 52 – 18 = _____
4. Find the average of 5, 9 and 4 = _____
5. Is $\frac{3}{10}$ the same as $\frac{6}{20}$? _____
6. 165 + 350 = _____
7. Is 435 divisible by 3? _____
8. 53 ÷ 6 = _____ remainder _____

9. Which is better value, 5 sweets for 65c or 4 sweets for 48c? _____
10. 60 x 70 = _____
11. Round 3·8 to the nearest whole number. _____
12. $\frac{4}{5} = \frac{}{10}$
13. What is the next number after 4,499? _____
14. 54, 48, 42, _____, _____

15. What is the value of 2 in 52,406? _____
16. 50 more than 1,236 = _____
17. 800 – 450 = _____
18. 3 x 3 = _____
19. 30 + 8 + 0·5 + 0·06 = _____
20. Circle the smaller fraction.
    $\frac{3}{5}$ $\frac{1}{2}$

/20

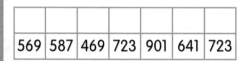

Code Cracker

Each problem has a letter. Solve the problem and put the letter into the grid to reveal the message! You may use your calculator.

A = 326 + 243 = _____
E = 658 + 65 = _____
O = 886 – 539 = _____
S = 987 – 518 = _____
N = 687 + 214 = _____
B = 231 + 356 = _____

C = 785 – 144 = _____
M = 843 – 296 = _____
T = 457 + 376 = _____
H = 354 + 264 + 111 = _____
G = 962 – 549 = _____
R = 658 – 215 = _____

W = 126 + 415 + 343 = _____
D = 872 – 256 = _____
F = 920 – 472 = _____
K = 232 + 123 + 342 = _____

WANTED!

569	587	469	723	901	641	723

547	569	697	723	469

833	729	723

729	723	569	443	833

413	443	347	884

448	347	901	616	723	443

Puzzle

Maria is 8 years old. John is 4 years older than Maria. Katie is 6 years younger than John. Robert is 10 years older than Katie. How old is Robert? _____

A Table Time

Beat the clock.

1. 2 x 7 = ____
2. 6 x 8 = ____
3. 9 x 9 = ____
4. 8 x 7 = ____
5. 3 x 6 = ____
6. 5 x 8 = ____
7. 1 x 7 = ____

8. 4 x 9 = ____
9. 7 x 6 = ____
10. 10 x 8 = ____
11. 0 x 7 = ____
12. 9 x 8 = ____
13. 3 x 8 = ____
14. 5 x 7 = ____

15. 2 x 6 = ____
16. 6 x 7 = ____
17. 0 x 8 = ____
18. 4 x 7 = ____
19. 7 x 7 = ____
20. 10 x 8 = ____

/20

B Try this

Splitting large numbers.

 Split large numbers

62 + 75

(60 + 70) + (2 + 5)

130 + 7 = 137

1. 34 + 42 = ____
2. 61 + 27 = ____
3. 49 + 58 = ____
4. 38 + 48 = ____
5. 75 + 81 = ____

6. 94 + 70 = ____
7. 84 + 39 = ____
8. 73 + 85 = ____
9. 29 + 49 = ____
10. 87 + 26 = ____

/10

C Mental Maths

In your head.

1. 9 a.m. = 09:00 hours ☐ 21:00 hours ☐
2. 6,450 + 225 = ____
3. 50 x 90 = ____
4. ⌐ Turn this shape 270° anticlockwise. Draw your answer ____
5. 2,239 < 2,204. True ☐ False ☐
6. 9 x 9 = ____
7. Write the next prime number after 13. ____
8. Will this shape tessellate? ____
9. 50% = $\frac{1}{2}$. True ☐ False ☐
10. 1, 3, 9, 27, ____
11. Write the number sixty eight thousand eight hundred and eight. ____

12. Name this 3D shape. ____
13. A rectangle has 4 right angles ☐ 4 reflex angles ☐
14. Circle the unit you would use to measure from Bray to Galway. metres kilometres
15. Write all the factors of 16.

____ ____ ____ ____ ____
16. Which is better value, 6 stickers for 36c or 3 stickers for 15c? ____
17. 70 + 80 = ____
18. €10·35 + €15·40 + €8·90 = ____
19. 8 ⌐96 = ____
20. 1·0 > 0·9. True ☐ False ☐

/20

D Vocabulary — Wordsearch.

1. The r_ _ _ _ _ is the line from centre of a circle to the circumference.

2. There are _ _ _ _ _ _ -_ _ _ _ hours in a day.

3. A regular 8 sided shape is called an _ _ _ _ _ _ _ _.

4. 1000 grammes = one _ _ _ _ _ _ _ _ _

5. $\frac{1}{8} + \frac{1}{8}$ = a _ _a_ _ _ _

6. $\frac{1}{2}$ = 50 _ _ _ _ _ _ _ _

7. A tin of beans is the shape of a _ _ _ _ _ _ _ _ _.

8. 0·008 = _ _ _ _ _ _ thousandths

9. 4 and 5 are f_ _ _ _ _ _ of 20.

h	w	t	h	j	q	u	t	c	d
z	e	u	n	d	e	r	w	y	r
s	m	o	m	f	y	c	e	l	e
u	m	c	p	a	z	q	n	i	t
i	a	t	e	c	i	v	t	n	r
d	r	a	r	t	e	u	y	d	a
a	g	g	c	o	i	p	f	e	u
r	o	o	e	r	g	z	o	r	q
z	l	n	n	s	h	u	u	e	l
i	i	q	t	g	t	q	r	y	g
l	k	h	e	z	p	y	d	x	i

E Mental Maths — In your head.

1. 7 p.m. = 07:00 ☐ 19:00 ☐

2. 2,506 + 4,285 = _ _ _ _

3. Round 6·8 to the nearest whole number. _ _ _ _

4. 54 ÷ 8 = _ _ _ _ remainder _ _ _ _

5. Circle the scales you would you use to weigh a teacup. kitchen scales bathroom scales

6. Write the next prime number after 23. _ _ _ _

7.  This shape is a _ _ _ _

8. A triangle has 3 acute angles ☐ obtuse angles ☐.

9. €20 – €11·50 = _ _ _ _

10. Circle the composite number. 11 15 19

11. 6 x 6 = _ _ _ _

12. Write the Roman numeral for 7 = _ _ _ _

13. Write the number seventy six thousand and three. _ _ _ _

14. Is 02:00 hours a.m. or p.m.? _ _ _ _

15. 100, 90, 70, 40, _ _ _ _

16. ▱ This shape is a _ _ _ _.

17. $\frac{7}{2}$ = 3 _ _ _ _

18. $7\frac{1}{2}$ = 7· _ _ _ _

19. 2,054 < 2,045. True ☐ False ☐

20. How many vertices does a triangular prism have? _ _ _ _

/20

F Puzzle — Problem of the week.

Jamie's ice cream parlour sells 5 different flavours of ice cream: vanilla, chocolate, strawberry, raspberry and nut. How many different combinations could you choose for double scoops? Remember you can get two scoops of the same ice cream! Hint: use a grid.

G Topic — Numbers. In your head.

1. Find the product of 18 and 20. ____
2. Odd number + odd number = ____
3. Even number + odd number = ____
4. Even number + even number = ____
5. Find the difference between 64 and 28. ____
6. Write the even numbers between 31 and 43.

   ____ ____ ____ ____

7. $240 \div 8 =$ ____
8. Write the odd numbers between 364 and

   372. ____ ____ ____ ____

9. $60 \times 3 =$ ____
10. Write the first 5 prime numbers.

    ____ ____ ____ ____ ____

11. Find the sum of 14, 6 and 9. ____

12. Write the factors of 8.

    ____ ____ ____ ____

13. $(810 \div 9) \div 10 =$ ____
14. What is the product of 11 and 50? ____
15. $(9 \times 3) \times 3 =$ ____
16. Write the first 5 multiples of 8.

    ____ ____ ____ ____ ____

17. $70 \times 80 =$ ____
18. What is the sum of the first 5 odd numbers?

    ____
19. $(44 \div 11) + 10 =$ ____
20. What is the sum of the first 4 even numbers? ____

/20

H Topic — Numbers. Problem solving. In your copy.

1. Katie bought 6 ice lollies. She got €1·40 change from €5·00. How much was each lolly? ____
2. A supermarket sold €30,270 worth of goods on Monday, €28,223 worth on Tuesday, €19,450 worth on Wednesday, €42,205 on Thursday and €51,290 on Friday. How much money did the supermarket take in? ____
3. (a) Take 58,296 from the sum of 34,216 and 48,265. ____

   (b) Add 18,091 to the difference between 83,291 and 58,636. ____
4. A shopkeeper sells 497 newspapers per week. How many does she sell in a year? ____

5. Mary has read 198 pages of *Adventure in Rome*. Brian has read 135 more.

   (a) How many has Brian read? ____

   (b) How many pages have they read between them? ____
6. Dad spent €1,200 on a table and 6 chairs. The table cost €360. How much was each chair? ____
7. Each week Anne drives 240 km to and from school (Monday to Friday). How far does she live from her school? ____

/7

I  Mental Maths

Beat the clock.

1. (4 x 7) + 13 = _____
2. (3 x 8) + 20 = _____
3. (7 x 6) + 15 = _____
4. (1 x 8) + 10 = _____
5. (6 x 7) + 12 = _____
6. (0 x 6) + 17 = _____
7. (8 x 7) + 20 = _____

8. (2 x 8) + 11 = _____
9. (1 x 7) + 19 = _____
10. (5 x 7) + 20 = _____
11. (7 x 7) + 10 = _____
12. (2 x 8) + 15 = _____
13. (10 x 6) + 11 = _____
14. (3 x 8) + 16 = _____

15. (8 x 8) + 19 = _____
16. (4 x 7) + 12 = _____
17. (9 x 6) + 18 = _____
18. (6 x 7) + 13 = _____
19. (9 x 8) + 17 = _____
20. (5 x 7) + 14 = _____

/20

J Code Cracker

Each problem has a letter. Solve the problem and put the letter into the grid to reveal the message!
You may use your calculator.

E = 342 + 147 = _____
I = 245 – 132 = _____
C = (658 – 326) ÷ 2 = _____
N = (147 + 215) – (48 + 17) = _____

S = 52,448 ÷ 176 = _____
B = 304·64 ÷ 4·48 = _____
X = 2,565 ÷ 15 = _____
R = (215 – 36) – 104 = _____
A = 25·8 x 15 = _____

H = (810 ÷ 90) ÷ 3 = _____
G = 245 x 4 = _____
O = 5·4 x 65 = _____
Y = 17 x 12 x 3 = _____

| 489 | 171 | 166 | 3 | 387 | 297 | 980 | 489 |

| 113 | 298 |

| 297 | 351 |

| 75 | 351 | 68 | 68 | 489 | 75 | 612 |

K  Puzzle

When this cube is made:

(a) Which shape is opposite the heart? _____

(b) Which shapes are next to the heart? _____

(c) Which shape is the arrow pointing to? _____

(d) Which shape is not next to the dot? _____

A Table Time — Beat the clock.

1. 3 x 8 = ____
2. 5 x 8 = ____
3. 9 x 9 = ____
4. 9 x 7 = ____
5. 8 x 8 = ____
6. 1 x 9 = ____
7. 2 x 8 = ____

8. 7 x 8 = ____
9. 2 x 9 = ____
10. 4 x 9 = ____
11. 4 x 8 = ____
12. 3 x 9 = ____
13. 6 x 8 = ____
14. 1 x 9 = ____

15. 8 x 6 = ____
16. 5 x 9 = ____
17. 0 x 8 = ____
18. 7 x 7 = ____
19. 10 x 8 = ____
20. 8 x 9 = ____

/20

B Try this — Making tens.

Making tens

Look for tens.
15 + 25 + 13
40 + 13 = 53

1. 16 + 14 + 12 = ____
2. 39 + 17 + 11 = ____
3. 23 + 27 + 16 = ____
4. 19 + 26 + 11 = ____
5. 48 + 6 + 22 = ____
6. 33 + 19 + 27 = ____
7. 13 + 37 + 15 = ____
8. 48 + 22 + 14 = ____

9. 56 + 2 + 34 = ____
10. 39 + 41 + 10 = ____
11. 16 + 12 + 24 = ____
12. 13 + 15 + 17 = ____
13. 16 + 15 + 15 = ____
14. 20 + 0 + 30 = ____
15. 15 + 15 + 24 = ____

/15

C Mental Maths — In your head.

1. 13:00 hours = ____ p.m.
2. There are ____ faces on a cone.
3. Round 11·9 to the nearest whole number. ____
4. Write $4\frac{1}{2}$ as an improper fraction. ____
5. Write $\frac{5}{2}$ as a mixed number. ____
6. 8 x 8 = ____
7. 25% = $\frac{3}{5}$. True ☐ False ☐
8. €50 – €35·50 = ____
9. 7 $\overline{)99}$ = ____ remainder ____
10. Which is heavier: 1 kg or 100 g? ____
11. 7,682 + 4,255 = ____

12. 90 x 70 = ____
13. Circle the prime number. 21 23 25
14. Will a circle tessellate? ____
15. Circle the smaller fraction. $\frac{3}{4}$ $\frac{5}{8}$
16. 0·7, 0·8, 0·9, ____, ____
17. Which unit would you use to weigh a packet of crisps? g ☐ kg ☐
18. Which is the longest? 100 cm ☐ 1 m ☐ 1·04 m ☐
19. Turn this shape 180° clockwise. ____
20. There are ____ edges on a triangular prism.

/20

D **Vocabulary**   Wordsearch.

1. A 5-sided shape is called a _ _ _ _ _ _ _ _ _.
2. (Length + width) x 2 = p_ _ _ _ _ _ _ _
3. If you turn in the direction of a clock's hands, you are going _ _ _ _ _ _ _ _ _ _.
4. The points of a compass are north, _ _ _ _ _, east, west.

5. 6, 9, 12, 3, 0. The average of these is _ _ _.
6. This is the net of a square _ _ _ _ _ _ _ _.
7. Shapes that fit together perfectly are said to t_ s_ e_ _ _ t_.
8. 23:00 hours = _ _ _ _ _ _ o'clock.

```
r  q  c  a  p  s  k  t  c  m
l  i  c  h  y  i  a  e  c  e
o  s  n  l  r  x  l  s  h  s
y  l  h  l  a  d  g  s  n  i
p  e  r  i  m  e  t  e  r  w
s  l  a  d  i  q  v  l  j  k
o  n  r  s  d  e  s  l  p  c
u  g  m  b  l  s  d  a  k  o
t  h  l  e  u  t  l  t  g  l
h  n  o  g  a  t  n  e  p  c
```

E **Mental Maths**   In your head.

1. 11:00 hours = _____ a.m.
2. 11 x 11 = _____
3. Circle the lighter. 250 g   25 kg
4. 3, 33, 333, 3333, _____, _____
5. €5 – €2·25 = _____
6. How many right angles in this shape? _____ How many obtuse angles? _____
7. Write $\frac{4}{3}$ as a mixed number. _____
8. Round 12·3 to the nearest whole number. _____
9. 40 x 60 = _____
10. $3\frac{3}{10}$ = 3· _____

11. 8, 17, 26, 35, _____
12. 2000 – 250 = _____
13. $\frac{1}{2} > \frac{1}{3} > \frac{1}{4}$. True ☐ False ☐
14. Circle the longer. 4 km   39·95 m
15. Name this shape. _____
16. The 3 angles in an equilateral triangle are acute ☐ reflex ☐ angles.
17. 300 + 900 + 3000 = _____
18. How many faces has a cuboid? _____
19. Circle the even number. 33 35 38
20. Circle the units you use to measure a spoonful of liquid. ml l

/20

F **Puzzle**   Problem of the week.

Which path leads to the square?

5 + 8 – 3 x 7 – 14 + 6
Start here

3 + 10 – 14 + 5 x 6 – 18
Start here

60

11 + 4 + 20 – 8 + 9 – 3

7 – 12 + 15 + 8 x 2 ÷ 10

G Topic — Money. In your head.

1. Draw the least number of coins needed to make up 69c. ____
2. €5 − €1·60 = ____
3. Which is better value, 4 apples for €1·40 or 6 apples for €2·46? ____
4. What is the total cost of 3 packets of nuts at 45c and 2 bottles of water at 80c? ____
5. I got 60c change from €5 when I bought 11 copies. How much did one copy cost? ____
6. €2·50 + €1·25 + €3·00 = ____
7. 6 pears cost €2·10. How much for 2 pears? ____
8. 5 kg sugar cost €3·50. How much for 1 kg? ____
9. I had €10. I have €3·50 left. How much did I spend? ____
10. €2·50 + €7·75 + €3·20 = ____
11. I had €5. I spent €1·35. What is my change? ____

12. €100 − €36 = ____
13. A pair of socks costs €2·50. How much for 7 pairs? ____
14. 6 cartons of juice cost €3·30. How much for 1 carton? ____
15. 9 snack bars cost €4·68. How much for 1 bar? ____
16. Which is better value: 8 pencils for €2·40 or 5 pencils for €2·00? ____
17. What is my change from €5 if I buy 5 apples at 35c each? ____
18. An adult's meal costs €40. A child's meal costs €20. Find the cost for 2 adults and 2 children. ____
19. List the coins needed to make up €3·35. ____
20. $\frac{1}{2}$ kg of sugar costs 85c. How much does 2 kg cost? ____

/20

H Topic — Money. Problem solving. In your copy.

1. Julie has €23·50. She earned €36·40. How much more does she need to buy a jacket for €79·99? ____
2. Tim worked for his dad in the shop for 8 hours one Saturday cleaning. Dad offered Tim €5·30 per hour or promised to buy him 2 CDs costing €26·50 each. Which was the better option for Tim? ____
3. (a) 3 apples cost 72c. How much for 2 apples? ____
   (b) Joan earned €75 for 3 nights babysitting. What would she earn for 5 nights? ____
   (c) 10 copies cost €3·60. How much for 30 copies? ____

4. The bus charges €350 to bring 30 children to a farm which costs €3·50 each and to a fun park which costs €5·50 per child. What is the total cost of the tour? ____
5. Dad earns €150 for an 8 hour day.
   (a) How much does he earn per hour? ____
   (b) How much does he earn for a week (5 days)? ____
6. Rebecca has €42·50 change out of €100 after buying 5 t-shirts. How much did she pay per t-shirt? ____

/6

I. Mental Maths

Beat the clock.

1. $(6 \times 8) - 2 =$ _____
2. $(1 \times 9) - 0 =$ _____
3. $(5 \times 8) - 5 =$ _____
4. $(7 \times 9) - 3 =$ _____
5. $(4 \times 8) - 1 =$ _____
6. $(3 \times 9) - 8 =$ _____
7. $(4 \times 9) - 2 =$ _____

8. $(1 \times 8) - 5 =$ _____
9. $(3 \times 8) - 6 =$ _____
10. $(10 \times 9) - 4 =$ _____
11. $(2 \times 8) - 1 =$ _____
12. $(7 \times 9) - 9 =$ _____
13. $(6 \times 11) - 10 =$ _____
14. $(1 \times 8) - 1 =$ _____

15. $(8 \times 8) - 8 =$ _____
16. $(5 \times 9) - 4 =$ _____
17. $(10 \times 8) - 6 =$ _____
18. $(6 \times 9) - 9 =$ _____
19. $(9 \times 8) - 7 =$ _____
20. $(10 \times 9) - 10 =$ _____

/20

J. Code Cracker

Each problem has a letter. Solve the problem and put the letter into the grid to reveal the message! You may use your calculator.

B $= \frac{1}{2}$ of $1{,}792 =$ _____

T $= (341 - 215) + 48 =$ _____

L $= 799 \cdot 2 \div 99 \cdot 9 =$ _____

H $= 315 + 316 + 317 =$ _____

V $= \frac{2}{3}$ of $906 =$ _____

E $= 74 \cdot 3 + 24 \cdot 6 =$ _____

R $= 796 + 121 =$ _____

A $= 125 + (\frac{4}{5}$ of $685) =$ _____

N $= (\frac{3}{8}$ of $648) - 24 =$ _____

896	98·9	174	174	98·9	917

8	673	174	98·9

174	948	673	219

219	98·9	604	98·9	917

K. Puzzle

Use the digits 0 to 9 to solve the number sentences. You can only use a digit once.

Hint: do the * first.

*$24 \div A = 12$

$B + C = 10$

*$15 \times D = 15$

$E \times F = 21$

$G - H = 4$

*$8 - I = 8$

*$7 \times J = 56$

A = _____   F = _____

B = _____   G = _____

C = _____   H = _____

D = _____   I = _____

E = _____   J = _____

A Table Time   Beat the clock.

1. 3 x 7 = ____
2. 5 x 9 = ____
3. 9 x 8 = ____
4. 7 x 10 = ____
5. 1 x 10 = ____
6. 10 x 7 = ____
7. 0 x 8 = ____

8. 2 x 8 = ____
9. 1 x 9 = ____
10. 6 x 7 = ____
11. 3 x 10 = ____
12. 8 x 7 = ____
13. 3 x 9 = ____
14. 4 x 8 = ____

15. 0 x 9 = ____
16. 10 x 9 = ____
17. 5 x 10 = ____
18. 4 x 10 = ____
19. 7 x 9 = ____
20. 11 x 8 = ____

/20

B Try this   Revise.

 **Revision**

Near doubles

Rounding. Splitting

Making tens

1. 93 + 47 = ____ est ____ ans
2. 380 + 97 = ____ est ____ ans
3. 24 + 75 = ____
4. 24 + 25 = ____
5. 16 + 14 + 42 = ____

6. 41 + 42 = ____
7. 83 + 84 = ____
8. 87 + 26 = ____
9. 49 + 11 + 20 = ____
10. 15 + 24 + 15 = ____

/10

C Mental Maths   In your head.

1. 09:30 hours = ____ a.m.
2. Write $5\frac{1}{3}$ as an improper fraction. ____
3. 955 + 3,005 = ____
4. 6·5 + 8·4 = ____
5. Round $7\frac{3}{4}$ to the nearest whole number. ____
6. 10$\overline{\smash{\big)}\,96}$ = ____ remainder ____
7. 11 x 11 = ____
8. A cube has ____ vertices.
9. 300 x 5 = ____
10. Which scales would you use to weigh an orange? Kitchen ☐ bathroom ☐
11. ◺ Name this triangle. ____
12. Write in order from the smallest to largest: 400 40,000 4,400 ____

13. What are the chances of rolling a 6 on a dice? ____ in 6
14. What are the chances of rolling an even number on a dice? ____ in 6
15. What are the chances of rolling an even number less than 5 on a dice? ____ in 6
16. ⊟ Turn this shape 270° clockwise. ____
17. ⬡ This shape is a ____.
18. The angles in the shape in question 17 are reflex angles ☐ obtuse angles ☐.
19. 15:15 = 3:15 a.m. ☐ 3:15 p.m. ☐
20. Circle positive 5.   15°   5°   ⁻5°

/20

D  | Wordsearch.

1. Name this 3D shape. _ _ _ _

2. A flat line is said to be _ _ _ _ _ _ _ _ _ _.

3. 150 – 90 = _ _ _ _ _

4. In 36·45 the 5 stands for 5 _ _ _ _ _ _ _ _ _.

5. A heptagon is a _ _ _ _ _-sided shape.

6. Twice the radius = _ _ _ _ _ _ _

7. This is the net of a triangular _ _ _ _ _.

8. 16 = 4 x 4. It is a _ _ _ _ _ _ number.

9. 17:30 = _ _ _ _-thirty p.m.

s	q	u	a	r	e	v	i	f	p
h	a	e	d	s	f	l	s	n	r
c	o	n	e	k	z	m	e	c	i
h	l	o	z	i	t	v	z	d	s
s	s	y	m	m	e	t	r	y	m
l	f	q	h	s	s	i	x	t	y
i	f	q	h	x	h	n	e	q	k
h	u	n	d	r	e	d	t	h	s
d	i	a	m	e	t	e	r	e	n
h	o	r	i	z	o	n	t	a	l

E Mental Maths — In your head.

1. 18:20 hours = _____ p.m.

2. Find the perimeter of a square with 4 cm sides. _____

3. Write $2\frac{3}{5}$ as an improper fraction. _____

4. 99 ÷ 10 = _____ remainder _____

5. A decagon has _____ sides.

6. 6 x 6 = _____

7. Circle the composite number. 4 5 7

8. Write $6\frac{7}{10}$ as a decimal. _____

9. Name this shape. _____

10. 23:59 hours = a.m. ☐ p.m. ☐

11. Is 517 divisible evenly by 3? _____

12. Circle the temperature positive 3. 13° 3° ⁻3°

13. 5cm What is the perimeter of this equilateral triangle? _____ cm

14. 11 x 6·5 = _____

15. Write $\frac{7}{3}$ as a mixed number. _____

16. Write in order from largest to smallest. 43,050 43,500 43,005 _____ _____ _____

17. 400 x 6 = _____

18. Is the letter A symmetrical? _____

19. 4·6 = $4\frac{}{10}$

20. 0·7, 0·4, 0·9, 0·6, _____, 0·8

/20

F Puzzle

Problem of the week.

Sudoku

Fill in the boxes so the numbers 1 to 9 appear once in each row, column and small grid.

6		3		4	2		9	
	9				6		5	
	5							1
		1	7			2	8	5
		8	4			1		
3	2	9			8	7		
	3		8					1
		5		9			2	
	8		2	1		6		

G Topic — Fractions. In your head.

1. $\frac{3}{4} = \frac{3}{10}$. True ☐ False ☐

2. Write $3\frac{1}{4}$ as an improper fraction. ____

3. Count in halves from 2 to $4\frac{1}{2}$.

   2, ____, ____, ____, ____, $4\frac{1}{2}$

4. $\frac{9}{2} = 4\frac{1}{\underline{}}$

5. $\frac{1}{3} = \frac{}{6}$

6. Write $\frac{23}{5}$ as a mixed number. ____

7. 1 unit = $\frac{}{10}$

8. $\frac{1}{3} = \frac{3}{12}$. True ☐ False ☐

9. Find the difference between $\frac{3}{4}$ of 20 and $\frac{1}{8}$ of 24. ____

10. $\frac{3}{7}$ of 49 = ____

11. $\frac{8}{9}$ ____ $\frac{2}{3}$. Insert <, > or =

12. What whole number is represented by $\frac{12}{3}$? ____

13. Count in quarters from 0 to $1\frac{3}{4}$.

   0, ____, ____, ____, ____, ____, ____, $1\frac{3}{4}$

14. $\frac{1}{2} = \frac{}{4} = \frac{}{8}$

15. Write $\frac{6}{18}$ in its lowest terms. ____

16. Write $2\frac{2}{3}$ as an improper fraction. ____

17. $\frac{1}{2}$ of 64 = ____

18. Take $\frac{1}{2}$ of 10 from $\frac{1}{4}$ of 32. ____

19. Add $\frac{1}{3}$ of 21 to $\frac{3}{5}$ of 35. ____

20. $\frac{3}{2}$ ____ $1\frac{1}{2}$. Insert <, > or =

$\diagup$20

H Topic — Fractions. Problem solving. In your copy.

1. John spent $\frac{1}{2}$ his money on a magazine and $\frac{1}{8}$ on sweets. What fraction of his money did he spend? ____

2. Emma got $\frac{2}{3}$ of her spellings correct. Mary got $\frac{7}{9}$ of her spellings right.

   (a) Who did better? ____

   (b) By how much, as a fraction? ____

3. (a) $\frac{1}{2}$ of 248 = ____   (b) $\frac{1}{3}$ of 927 = ____

   (c) $\frac{1}{4}$ of 256 = ____   (d) $\frac{3}{4}$ of 724 = ____

   (e) $\frac{5}{8}$ of 528 = ____

4. Mrs Conway planted half her flowers on Saturday morning. If she planted 34 flowers, how many had she at first? ____

5. Bill has saved €52 which is $\frac{1}{3}$ of what he needs to buy a games console. How much is the console? ____

6. Mary has 15 marbles. She lost 3 playing against her friend. What fraction of her marbles did she lose? ____

7. Seán bought 12 pieces of fruit. $\frac{1}{4}$ were apples, $\frac{1}{3}$ were pears and the rest were kiwis. How many kiwis did he buy? ____

8. $\frac{3}{4}$ of a number is 456. Find $\frac{5}{8}$ of the number. ____

$\diagup$8

Mental Maths

Beat the clock.

1. (3 x 1) – 0 = ___
2. (7 x 7) + 5 = ___
3. (5 x 8) + 14 = ___
4. (9 x 9) + 19 = ___
5. (7 x 10) – 11 = ___
6. (6 x 2) – 4 = ___
7. (9 x 8) + 15 = ___
8. (4 x 6) – 3 = ___
9. (1 x 3) + 18 = ___
10. (8 x 9) – 12 = ___
11. (2 x 4) – 3 = ___
12. (0 x 10) – 0 = ___
13. (10 x 3) + 16 = ___
14. (4 x 5) + 10 = ___
15. (3 x 2) + 5 = ___
16. (5 x 4) – 19 = ___
17. (6 x 5) – 7 = ___
18. (2 x 6) + 20 = ___
19. (8 x 1) + 14 = ___
20. (1 x 7) – 2 = ___

/20

J Code Cracker

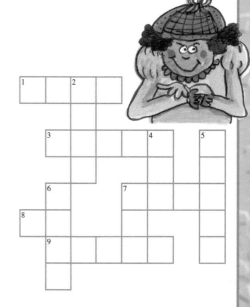

Across
1. 860 + 559
3. 12,807 + 9362 + 46 + 587
7. 32 x 34
8. The average of 77, 28, 49 and 58
9. Round 53,678 to the nearest 100

Down
2. 2000 – 272
4. $80 \times 2\frac{1}{2}$
5. Write $\frac{7}{8}$ as a decimal
6. (48 + 87) x 10
7. The degrees in a straight angle

K Puzzle

Last week Mary, John, Peter and Kate went out for a pizza. They ordered a large pizza with 8 slices. The pizza cost €16. Mary said each should pay €2 because €16 ÷ 8 is €2. Kate said she was wrong and that they each owed €4. Who was right and why? ___

A. Table Time — Beat the clock.

1. (18 ÷ 2) x 1 = _____
2. (27 ÷ 3) x 3 = _____
3. (21 ÷ 3) x 5 = _____
4. (20 ÷ 0) x 2 = _____
5. (32 ÷ 4) x 4 = _____
6. (33 ÷ 3) x 1 = _____
7. (16 ÷ 2) x 0 = _____

8. (20 ÷ 2) x 8 = _____
9. (36 ÷ 3) x 10 = _____
10. (40 ÷ 4) x 5 = _____
11. (14 ÷ 2) x 7 = _____
12. (18 ÷ 3) x 3 = _____
13. (36 ÷ 4) x 8 = _____
14. (22 ÷ 2) x 5 = _____

15. (15 ÷ 3) x 1 = _____
16. (20 ÷ 4) x 2 = _____
17. (28 ÷ 2) x 5 = _____
18. (6 ÷ 3) x 8 = _____
19. (12 ÷ 2) x 4 = _____
20. (16 ÷ 4) x 9 = _____

/20

B. Try this — Look for patterns.

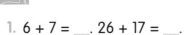

Look for patterns

8 + 4 = 12
18 + 14 = 32
38 + 24 = 62

1. 6 + 7 = __. 26 + 17 = __.
   46 + 27 = __
2. 5 + 9 = __. 35 + 19 = __.
   45 + 29 = __
3. 9 + 8 = __. 19 + 18 = __.
   89 + 8 = __
4. 8 + 6 = __. 38 + 26 = __.
   58 + 36 = __

5. 2 + 6 = __. 22 + 26 = __.
   32 + 46 = __
6. 3 + 8 = __. 33 + 28 = __.
   43 + 48 = __
7. 6 + 5 = __. 36 + 15 = __.
   66 + 25 = __
8. 9 + 7 = __. 39 + 17 = __.
   59 + 27 = __

/8

C. Mental Maths — In your head.

1. 00:01 hours = a.m. ☐ p.m. ☐
2. ⬚ This is the net of a _____
3. 11·6 + 6·3 = _____
4. Write $5\frac{1}{3}$ as an improper fraction. _____
5. €10·50 + €3·75 + €8·25 = _____
6. 12 x 12 = _____
7. Is 406 divisible evenly by 3? _____
8. ⬚ 4cm Find the perimeter of this
   8cm
   rectangle. _____ cm
9. Is 12 a multiple of 3? _____
10. What is the product of 5 and 8? _____

11. The angles in a regular hexagon are all
    _____ angles. ⬡
12. A sphere has _____ faces.
13. Circle positive 4.   11°c   4°c   ⁻2°c
14. Circle the shortest length. 400 mm 0·45 m 85 cm
15. Write $\frac{9}{5}$ as a mixed number. _____
16. Circle the composite number. 18   23   29
17. Write the Roman numeral for 11. _____
18. 0·3, 0·7, _____, 1·5
19. Is 3 a multiple of 9? _____
20. 500 x 8 = _____

/20

D  Vocabulary

Wordsearch.

1. A triangle with two sides the same length is called an __s__s__ __ __ __ __ triangle.

2. An equilateral triangle has three sides the same __ __ __ __ __ __.

3. A triangle that has no sides of equal length is called a s__ __ __ __ __ __ triangle.

4. An angle less than 90° is an __ __ __ __ __ angle.

5. An angle greater than 90° but less than 180° is an __ __ __ __ __ __ __ angle.

6. A square has all 4 __ __ __ __ __ the same length.

7. A square pushed out of shape is called a rh__ __ __ __ __.

```
x  j  q  y  c  k  p  w  s  h
d  o  a  d  x  e  u  s  r  c
v  r  t  c  h  t  g  n  e  l
s  i  s  o  s  c  e  l  e  s
m  c  r  l  n  l  d  o  u  e
u  u  a  c  p  k  z  b  s  t
s  n  c  l  v  x  m  t  e  u
h  t  n  w  e  o  c  u  d  c
l  w  c  a  h  n  h  s  i  a
o  z  v  r  o  j  e  e  s  p
```

E Mental Maths

In your head.

1. 10:35 hours = _____ a.m.

2. A square pyramid has _____ vertices.

3. Draw a symmetrical letter. _____

4. How many seconds in $1\frac{1}{4}$ minutes? _____

5. 9,996, 9,997, 9,998, _____, _____

6. Write $5\frac{1}{2}$ as a decimal. _____

7. 15·6 + 5·9 = _____

8. 94 ÷ 4 = _____ remainder _____

9. 600 x 3 = _____

10. 30% = $\frac{1}{3}$. True ☐ False ☐

11. $\frac{4}{10}$ < $\frac{1}{5}$. True ☐ False ☐

12. Is 15 a multiple of 5? _____

13. 1505 > 1550. True ☐ False ☐

14. Round 14·5 to the nearest whole. _____

15. How many days in 9 weeks? _____

16. How many sides has a nonagon? _____

17. 8·9 cm = _____ mm

18. 15:45 hours = $\frac{1}{4}$ to _____ p.m.

19. What is the difference between 29 and 15? _____

20. Name this triangle. _____

/20

F Puzzle

Problem of the week.

Arrange 10 x's along the edge of this rectangle so that there are an equal number of x's on each side.

Topic G · 2D Shapes. In your head.

1. The three angles of a triangle add up to _____ °.

2. 7cm /\ 7cm Find the perimeter of this shape.
   8cm _____

3. What do you call a shape with 8 sides all the same length? R_____ O_____

4. In 2D what does the D mean? _____

5. Will this shape tessellate? ⬠▷ _____

6. A rhombus has 4 right angles.
   True ☐ False ☐

7. If the radius of a circle is 5 cm, what is the diameter? _____

8. A quadrilateral has 6 sides. True ☐ False ☐

9. The angles of a quadrilateral add up to 180° ☐ 360° ☐ 90° ☐.

10. A regular decagon has sides measuring 5 cm. What is its perimeter? _____

11. Name this shape. ⬡ _____

12. How many pairs of parallel lines in a square? _____

13. If the length of the side of a square is 8 cm, what is its perimeter? _____

14. The sum of the three sides of a scalene triangle is 12 cm. One side is 4 cm, the other is 3 cm. What is the length of the third side? _____

15. A regular pentagon has 5 o_____ angles.

16. Name this shape. _____ ▱

17. A square is a rectangle, a rectangle is a square. True ☐ False ☐

18. Calculate the size of angle a. /a\ 50 50 _____

19. A rectangle is a regular polygon. True ☐ False ☐

20. A heptagon has 6 ☐ 7 ☐ 8 ☐ sides.

/20

Topic H · 2D Shapes. Complete this table. In your copy.

	△	⊡	▭	△	⬠	▱	⬡	⬡
Name of shape								
Number of angles								
Type of angles								
Does it tessellate?								
Number of axes of symmetry								

/5

Mental Maths

Beat the clock.

Baker Street

1. $\frac{1}{4}$ of 32 = _____

2. $\frac{2}{3}$ of 21 = _____

3. $\frac{2}{9}$ of 36 = _____

4. $\frac{5}{6}$ of 42 = _____

5. $\frac{3}{6}$ of 72 = _____

6. $\frac{1}{2}$ of 14 = _____

7. $\frac{1}{10}$ of 70 = _____

8. $\frac{2}{5}$ of 55 = _____

9. $\frac{5}{8}$ of 48 = _____

10. $\frac{3}{7}$ of 56 = _____

11. $\frac{2}{11}$ of 44 = _____

12. $\frac{2}{8}$ of 16 = _____

13. $\frac{1}{3}$ of 30 = _____

14. $\frac{3}{4}$ of 56 = _____

15. $\frac{8}{10}$ of 50 = _____

16. $\frac{1}{2}$ of 66 = _____

17. $\frac{4}{9}$ of 81 = _____

18. $\frac{3}{12}$ of 144 = _____

19. $\frac{6}{7}$ of 28 = _____

20. $\frac{3}{5}$ of 15 = _____

 /20

J Code Cracker

Each problem has a letter. Solve the problem and put the letter into the grid to reveal the message! You may use your calculator.

A = 436 x 2 = _____

O = (459 + 636) – 147 = _____

D = 241 x 4 = _____

H = $\frac{6}{9}$ of 909 = _____

M = 748 – 134 – 198 = _____

Y = 30·0 x (18 ÷ 2) = _____

R = 69·5 – 15·5 = _____

T = 63 x 11 = _____

F = 1,987 – (28 x 59) = _____

L = 435 + 217 + 18 = _____

N = (63 x 42) – 2,135 = _____

I = (795 x 5) ÷ 15 = _____

S = (214 ÷ 2) x 7 = _____

E = (5 x 90) ÷ 10 = _____

P = 144 ÷ 12 = _____

872

335	948	948	670

872	511	964

606	265	749

416	948	511	45	270

872	54	45

749	948	948	511

12	872	54	693	45	964

K Puzzle

Draw this house without picking up your pencil or going over any line twice.

A Table Time — Beat the clock.

1. $(12 \div 4) + 7 =$ ____
2. $(9 \div 3) + 2 =$ ____
3. $(25 \div 5) + 6 =$ ____
4. $(24 \div 4) + 13 =$ ____
5. $(24 \div 6) + 5 =$ ____
6. $(30 \div 5) + 8 =$ ____
7. $(15 \div 3) + 4 =$ ____

8. $(20 \div 4) + 3 =$ ____
9. $(36 \div 6) + 9 =$ ____
10. $(45 \div 5) + 2 =$ ____
11. $(21 \div 3) + 0 =$ ____
12. $(18 \div 6) + 1 =$ ____
13. $(32 \div 4) + 20 =$ ____
14. $(36 \div 4) + 10 =$ ____

15. $(55 \div 5) + 12 =$ ____
16. $(20 \div 5) + 14 =$ ____
17. $(27 \div 3) + 15 =$ ____
18. $(48 \div 6) + 13 =$ ____
19. $(60 \div 6) + 17 =$ ____
20. $(30 \div 3) + 18 =$ ____

/20

B Try this — Multiplying by 10, 100, 1,000.

X by 10, 100, 1,000

$19 \times \underline{10} = 19\underline{0}$
$19 \times \underline{100} = 19\underline{00}$
$19 \times \underline{1,000} = 19,\underline{000}$

1. $37 \times 10 =$ ____
2. $43 \times 100 =$ ____
3. $91 \times 10 =$ ____
4. $20 \times 1,000 =$ ____
5. $6 \times 100 =$ ____
6. $101 \times 10 =$ ____
7. $153 \times 1,000 =$ ____
8. $9 \times 1,000 =$ ____

9. $12 \times 10 =$ ____
10. $85 \times 1,000 =$ ____
11. $48 \times 100 =$ ____
12. $3 \times 10 =$ ____
13. $69 \times 100 =$ ____
14. $247 \times 10 =$ ____
15. $375 \times 100 =$ ____

/15

C Mental Maths — In your head.

1. 09:55 hours = ____ a.m.
2. 3·5 km = ____ m
3. $300 \times 8 =$ ____
4. 0·2, 2·0, 20, ____, 2,000
5. Write 3·7 as a fraction. ____
6. Is 12 a multiple of 4? ____
7. How many vertical lines in a square? ____

8. Turn this shape 180° clockwise. ____
9. $83 \div 7 =$ ____ remainder ____
10. 17:40 hours = 20 to ____ p.m.

11. A square-based pyramid has ____ edges.
12. Write the temperature 4 degrees. ____ °C
13. 2,300 > 2,333. True ☐ False ☐
14. $\frac{3}{4} < 1$. True ☐ False ☐
15. 300, 600, 400, 700, 500, ____
16. Name this shape. ____
17. Is 507 divisible evenly by 3? ____
18. Write in order from largest to smallest.
    74,803 47,803 74,038 ____
19. Circle the prime number. 33 35 37
20. 10 kg = ____ g

/20

D. Vocabulary — Wordsearch.

1. The period of time between midnight and midday is ___ time.
2. 60 seconds = 1 _ _ _ _ _ _
3. The number on the top line of a fraction is called a _ _ _ _ _ _ _ _ _ _.
4. The points on a compass are north, south, _ _ _ _ and west.
5. 8 and 9 are factors of _ _ _ _ _ _ _-two.
6. 1000 years = a _ _ _l_ _n_ _ _.
7. 1_ _ _ _ _ _ _ _ _ = 1000 metres
8. 19:00 hours = _ _ _ _ _ o'clock.
9. 90° = a _ _ _ _ _ angle
10. A 10 sided shape is called a _ _ _ _ _ _ _ _.

t	s	q	l	k	u	k	x	k	j
t	t	h	g	i	r	s	p	e	n
m	q	c	a	r	l	r	d	t	u
m	i	l	l	e	n	n	i	u	m
a	n	o	g	a	c	e	d	n	e
m	e	a	s	t	b	m	p	i	r
e	y	t	n	e	v	e	s	m	a
n	v	a	t	n	e	v	e	s	t
k	i	l	o	m	e	t	r	e	o
o	u	g	k	i	h	m	l	j	r

E. Mental Maths — In your head.

1. 14:25 hours = ____ p.m.
2. 18·2 + 23·7 = ____
3. This shape is a triangular prism ☐ rectangular pyramid ☐ triangular pyramid ☐.
4. Is 17 a multiple of 4? ____
5. Write $4\frac{1}{8}$ as an improper fraction. ____
6. How many horizontal lines in a regular pentagon? ____
7. 55 + ____ = 120
8. What are the chances of rolling 3 on a dice? ____ in ____
9. Write the Roman numeral for 8. ____
10. What are the chances of rolling a multiple of 3 on a dice? ____ in ____
11. What are the chances of rolling a number including and lower than 4 on a dice? ____ in ____
12. What are the chances of rolling an odd number on a dice? ____ in ____
13. Will this shape tessellate? ____
14. What is the first prime number? ____
15. This is the net of ____

/20

F. Puzzle — Problem of the week.

The train from Dublin to Athlone stops only 3 times. After $\frac{1}{8}$ of the journey it stops to let off some passengers. It then travels 30 km and stops again, bringing it to the halfway point of its journey. The train then continues until it reaches Athlone. How long was the journey? ____

Topic

Time. In your head.

1. How many minutes in $\frac{3}{4}$ of an hour? _____

2. Write 7:45 a.m. in 24 hour time. _____

3. Write 00:35 hours in 12 hour time. _____

4. What time is 25 minutes later than 7:20 p.m.? _____

5. What time is 20 minutes earlier than 6:10 a.m.? _____

6. How many seconds in $1\frac{1}{4}$ minutes? _____

7. What date is one week later than 25th July? _____

8. How many weeks in a year and a half? _____

9. How many minutes in 2 hours 45 minutes? _____

10. Write the time $9\frac{3}{4}$ hours after 10:35 p.m. _____

11. Write the time 15 minutes before 7:05 a.m. _____

12. Write the time 25 minutes after 6:40 a.m. _____

13. How many days from 17th March to 4th April, including both days? _____

14. Write 16 minutes to 9 at night in the 24 hour clock. _____

15. Write 12 minutes past midnight in the 24 hour clock. _____

16. Write 12:25 hours using a.m. or p.m. _____

17. How many minutes in $2\frac{1}{2}$ hours? _____

18. How many hours and minutes from 05:20 to 06:30? _____

19. What date is one week earlier than 4th October? _____

20. A film starts at 8:10 p.m. It is $2\frac{1}{2}$ hours long. What time does it finish at? _____

/20

Topic

Time. Problem solving. In your copy.

1.

hrs min	hrs min	hrs min	hrs min
2:27		4:36	
3:19	3:21	1:23	5:28
+ 1:48	− 1:47	+ 4:51	− 3:42

2. A shop opened at 07:45 and closed at 18:30 each day. How many hours and minutes was it open for each day? _____

3. How many hours and minutes are there from:
   (a) 03:42 to 07:20? _____
   (b) 05:38 to 11:25? _____
   (c) 11:15 to 15:08? _____
   (d) 14:27 to 23:18? _____

4. A film started at 17:48 and lasted 1 hour 55 minutes. At what time did it finish? _____

5. (a) $3\frac{1}{2}$ hours + 4 hours 36 minutes + $1\frac{1}{4}$ hours = _____ hours _____ minutes
   (b) $2\frac{1}{3}$ hours + $4\frac{3}{4}$ hours + 2 hours 10 minutes = _____ hours _____ minutes
   (c) $1\frac{1}{4}$ hours + 3 hours 20 minutes + 90 minutes = _____ hours _____ minutes

6. A doctor's surgery was open from 09:30 to 12:15 and later from 13:30 to 17:30 each day. For how many hours and minutes was the surgery open? _____

/6

I. Mental Maths

Beat the clock.

Find the whole number if:

1. $\frac{1}{2}$ = 46. _____
2. $\frac{1}{3}$ = 156. _____
3. $\frac{5}{6}$ = 675. _____
4. $\frac{1}{4}$ = 140. _____
5. $\frac{2}{3}$ = 120. _____
6. $\frac{8}{9}$ = 2,792. _____
7. $\frac{5}{9}$ = 790. _____

8. $\frac{11}{12}$ = 99. _____
9. $\frac{6}{7}$ = 1,476. _____
10. $\frac{1}{3}$ = 90. _____
11. $\frac{3}{8}$ = 450. _____
12. $\frac{4}{5}$ = 1,284. _____
13. $\frac{1}{5}$ = 150. _____
14. $\frac{3}{4}$ = 2,766. _____

15. $\frac{1}{6}$ = 248. _____
16. $\frac{1}{4}$ = 48. _____
17. $\frac{3}{7}$ = 480. _____
18. $\frac{1}{9}$ = 355. _____
19. $\frac{7}{8}$ = 2,429. _____
20. $\frac{8}{10}$ = 480. _____

/20

J. Code Cracker

Each problem has a letter. Solve the problem and put the letter into the grid to reveal the message! You may use your calculator.

E = 265 + 324 = _____
W = 120 x 5 = _____
T = 36·5 x 8 = _____
A = (58·65 x 4) – 0·6 = _____
Y = 665·9 – 210·9 = _____

I = (54 x 53) – 2,000 = _____
P = (8,391 + 53,268) – 61,320 = _____
N = (795 ÷ 5) x 3 = _____
H = 24·5 x 16 = _____

C = $\frac{5}{6}$ of 1,002 = _____
S = $\frac{1}{2}$ (325 + 653) = _____
M = 0·9 + 9 + 0·09 = _____
L = 3 + 23 + 33 = _____

600	392	589	477

292	392	589

835	234	292	489

234	600	234	455

292	392	589

9·99	862	835	589

600	862	59	59

339	59	234	455

K. Puzzle

Move only 3 dots to turn this triangular pattern upside down.

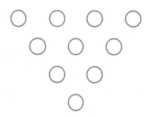

A Table Time

Beat the clock.

1. (36 ÷ 6) ÷ 2 = ____
2. (48 ÷ 8) ÷ 3 = ____
3. (42 ÷ 7) ÷ 6 = ____
4. (35 ÷ 5) ÷ 1 = ____
5. (8 ÷ 8) ÷ 0 = ____
6. (24 ÷ 6) ÷ 2 = ____
7. (25 ÷ 5) ÷ 1 = ____

8. (28 ÷ 7) ÷ 4 = ____
9. (18 ÷ 6) ÷ 3 = ____
10. (24 ÷ 8) ÷ 1 = ____
11. (49 ÷ 7) ÷ 7 = ____
12. (50 ÷ 5) ÷ 5 = ____
13. (80 ÷ 8) ÷ 10 = ____
14. (54 ÷ 6) ÷ 3 = ____

15. (15 ÷ 5) ÷ 0 = ____
16. (56 ÷ 7) ÷ 4 = ____
17. (30 ÷ 6) ÷ 5 = ____
18. (56 ÷ 8) ÷ 7 = ____
19. (63 ÷ 7) ÷ 3 = ____
20. (30 ÷ 5) ÷ 3 = ____

/20

B Try this

Multiplying by 10 and by 100.

x by 10 and 100
x 10: move the · one space to the right
x 100: move the · two spaces to the right

1. 2·46 x 10 = ____
2. 2·975 x 100 = ____
3. 16·143 x 100 = ____
4. 85·35 x 100 = ____
5. 2·43 x 10 = ____

6. 5·84 x 100 = ____
7. 61·4 x 10 = ____
8. 29·8 x 10 = ____
9. 36·41 x 100 = ____
10. 0·096 x 100 = ____

/10

C Mental Maths

In your head.

1. Write 07:35 hours in a.m./p.m. time. ____
2. 2 x a = 6 + 4. a = ____
3. How many seconds in $2\frac{1}{2}$ minutes? ____
4. 105 ÷ 10 = ____ remainder ____
5. 85 + ____ = 170
6. 1, 3, 9, ____
7. What is 50% of a fortnight? ____
8. What kind of angle does 68° make?
   Acute ☐ obtuse ☐ right ☐
9. How many days in July? ____
10. Is 22 a multiple of 3? ____
11. This shape is a pentagonal prism ☐
    triangular prism ☐ pentagonal pyramid ☐.

12. Write in order from largest to smallest.
    82,496 82,964 82,946 ____
13. Circle the symmetrical letters. F S H J A
14. 1, 2, 3, 5 and 15 are factors of 15.
    True ☐ False ☐
15. 1,200 mm = ____ m
16. ____ + 95 = 130
17. 2, 4, 8, 16, ____
18. Find the perimeter of this shape. ____ 3 3 3 3 3 3cm
19. Turn this shape 90°
    anticlockwise. ____
20. Name this 3D shape. ____

/20

Vocabulary

Wordsearch.

1. The 6 in 46,234 stands for six _ _ _ _ _ _ _.

2. 14 days = one _ _ _ _ _ _ _ _ _

3. Double 55 = one hundred and _ _ _

4. 17 + 36 + 29 = _ _ _ _ _ _-two

5. The time between midday and midnight is _ _ time.

6. €85·00 – €35·00 = _ _ _ _ _ euro

7. The 2 in 241,987 stands for two _ _ _ _ _ _ _ thousand.

8. The d_ _ _ _ _ _ _ _ between 6 and 9 is 3.

9. 10 mm = 1 _ _ _ _ _ _ _ _ _ _

```
g d e r d n u h t x
p m j p i g z t e q
t p t h o u s a n d
d i f f e r e n c e
e y t h g i e u d f
c i d c t u p p k x
a r l f i f t y g j
d l g g t h j e h l
e f o r t n i g h t
c e n t i m e t r e
```

Mental Maths

In your head.

1. 22:20 hours = ____ p.m.
2. $1 > \frac{4}{5}$. True ☐ False ☐
3. What are the factors of 4? ____ ____ ____
4. ____ + 45 = 135
5. Write $\frac{2}{10}$ as a decimal. ____
6. 8 + 2 = y + 5. y = ____
7. Area = length x width = ____ cm² 8cm / 4cm
8. Find the perimeter of the shape in question 7. ____ cm
9. Simplify $\frac{3}{6}$ = ____
10. Name this shape. ____

11. In 5,678, 5 stands for 500 ☐ 5,000 ☐.
12. $\frac{10}{12} = \frac{5}{\underline{\quad}}$
13. Circle the number negative 2. -3 -2 -1 0 1 2
14. What date is the day after 31st March? ____
15. 50% of 100 = ____
16. Name this shape. ____
17. What time is 20 minutes before 11:10? ____
18. 72,009 = ____ + 2,000 + 9
19. 72 minutes = 1 hour ____ minutes
20. What three coins make 35c? ____

/20

Puzzle

Problem of the week.

Draw this shape into the grid so that every square is filled and each shape tessellates.

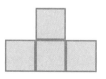

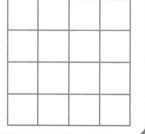

G Topic — Decimals. In your head.

1. What does the 4 stand for in 32·48? _____

2. Write $4\frac{17}{100}$ as a decimal. _____

3. Write 0·9 as a fraction. _____

4. Which is greatest: 0·21, 1·09 or 1·009? _____

5. Write in order, starting with the largest.

   2·03 1·43 3·31 _____ _____ _____

6. What is the value of 7 in these numbers?

   7·14 _____ 3·74 _____ 2·07 _____ 71·36 _____

7. $\frac{113}{1000} = \frac{}{10} + \frac{}{100} + \frac{}{1000}$

8. 0·4 + 0·37 = _____

9. 1 – 0·36 = _____

10. 3 + 2·5 + 0·06 = _____

11. 4·07 = 4 + $\frac{}{10}$ + $\frac{}{100}$

12. Write $\frac{17}{10}$ as a decimal. _____

13. Write 0·08 as a fraction. _____

14. 0·01 > 0·011. True ☐ False ☐

15. Put in order, starting with the smallest.

    3·19 3·91 2·008 _____ _____ _____

16. $\frac{15}{1000} = \frac{}{10} + \frac{}{100} + \frac{}{1000}$

17. 7 – 2·4 = _____

18. Write 0·55 as a fraction in its lowest terms.

    _____

19. Write as decimals and subtract the smaller from the larger. $\frac{1}{2}$ $\frac{3}{4}$ _____ _____ _____

20. Write as decimals and add. $\frac{1}{2}$ $\frac{7}{10}$

    _____ _____ _____

/20

H Topic — Decimals. Problem solving. In your copy.

1. Write the following numbers as decimals and subtract the smaller number from the bigger number.

   (a) $\frac{1}{2}$ $\frac{1}{4}$ _____   (b) $\frac{4}{5}$ $\frac{3}{4}$ _____

   (c) $\frac{1}{2}$ $\frac{9}{10}$ _____   (d) $7\frac{3}{10}$ $7\frac{3}{4}$ _____

   (e) $\frac{7}{8}$ $\frac{1}{2}$ _____

2. Two parcels are weighed. Parcel A = 20·08 kg. Parcel B = 7·395 kg. How much heavier is Parcel A than Parcel B? _____

3. Write these fractions as decimals and add.

   $2\frac{73}{100}$ $2\frac{9}{10}$ $8\frac{57}{1000}$ $56\frac{1}{2}$ _____

4. By how much is 23·7 greater than 12·345?

   _____

5. By how much is the 7 in 57·26 greater than the 7 in 2·375? _____

6. John weighs 42·5 kg. Sam is 3·52 kg heavier than John. What is their total weight? _____

7. Sheila weighs 51·36 kg. She is 1·75 kg heavier than Elaine. Elaine is 3·54 kg heavier than Katie.

   (a) What does Katie weigh? _____

   (b) What is the total weight of the 3 girls?

   _____

/7

Beat the clock.

Write these fractions as decimals.

1. $\frac{1}{10}$ = _____
2. $\frac{54}{100}$ = _____
3. $\frac{6}{10}$ = _____
4. $\frac{2}{100}$ = _____
5. $\frac{8}{100}$ = _____
6. $\frac{17}{100}$ = _____
7. $\frac{13}{1000}$ = _____
8. $\frac{3}{100}$ = _____
9. $\frac{5}{1000}$ = _____
10. $\frac{73}{100}$ = _____
11. $\frac{21}{100}$ = _____
12. $\frac{59}{100}$ = _____
13. $\frac{37}{1000}$ = _____
14. $\frac{34}{100}$ = _____
15. $\frac{61}{1000}$ = _____
16. $\frac{75}{100}$ = _____
17. $\frac{8}{1000}$ = _____
18. $\frac{29}{100}$ = _____
19. $\frac{457}{1000}$ = _____
20. $\frac{3}{10}$ = _____

/20

 Code Cracker

Each problem has a letter. Solve the problem and put the letter into the grid to reveal the message! You may use your calculator.

E = 43·5 x 8 = _____
A = (217 ÷ 7) x 8 = _____
P = (369 ÷ 9) x 7 = _____
Y = 29·6 ÷ 2 = _____
S = 23·5 + 36·5 = _____
O = 79·58 + 22·42 + 16·0 = _____
C = ((50 x 8) ÷ 10) + 6 = _____
W = (68 + 82) x 6 = _____
D = 28·7 + 41·3 + 69·0 = _____
N = 25·8 x 15 = _____
L = 74·3 x 8 – 125·4 = _____
K = 578·3 – 246·3 = _____
T = 12·5 x 14 = _____
H = (17 x 156) ÷ 4 = _____
R = (24 ÷ 12) x 317 = _____

248	387

248	287	287	469	348

248

139	248	14·8

332	348	348	287	60

175	663	348

139	118	46	175	118	634

248	900	248	14·8

 Puzzle

Start at square 8. Move through 5 squares to make a path that adds up to 50. You can move up, down, sideways and diagonally.

4	20	17	9
8	19	6	15
12	3	0	5
11	17	2	13

A Table Time

Beat the clock.

1. (45 ÷ 9) × 2 = ____
2. (64 ÷ 8) × 3 = ____
3. (80 ÷ 10) × 1 = ____
4. (72 ÷ 8) × 4 = ____
5. (56 ÷ 7) × 2 = ____
6. (63 ÷ 9) × 5 = ____
7. (40 ÷ 10) × 3 = ____

8. (40 ÷ 8) × 6 = ____
9. (49 ÷ 7) × 4 = ____
10. (54 ÷ 9) × 7 = ____
11. (24 ÷ 8) × 6 = ____
12. (27 ÷ 9) × 5 = ____
13. (81 ÷ 9) × 9 = ____
14. (8 ÷ 8) × 6 = ____

15. (0 ÷ 10) × 6 = ____
16. (32 ÷ 8) × 9 = ____
17. (63 ÷ 7) × 8 = ____
18. (100 ÷ 10) × 7 = ____
19. (56 ÷ 8) × 10 = ____
20. (9 ÷ 9) × 8 = ____

/20

B Try this

Dividing by 10.

Dividing by 10

$14 ÷ 10 = 1·4$
$135 ÷ 10 = 13·5$
$24·3 ÷ 10 = 2·43$

1. 700 ÷ 10 = ____
2. 34·3 ÷ 10 = ____
3. 4983·6 ÷ 10 = ____
4. 490 ÷ 10 = ____
5. 840 ÷ 10 = ____

6. 290 ÷ 10 = ____
7. 29·86 ÷ 10 = ____
8. 2804 ÷ 10 = ____
9. 27 ÷ 10 = ____
10. 8100 ÷ 10 = ____

/10

C Mental Maths

In your head.

1. Write 8 p.m. in 24 hour time. ____
2. 7 × 7 = ____
3. $10\% = \frac{10}{100} = 0·$____
4. 7, 14, 21, ____, ____
5. Write a composite number between 10 and 20. ____
6. Is 555 divisible by 5? ____
7. Write the Roman numeral for 15. ____
8.  How many pairs of parallel lines in this shape? ____
9. Simplify $\frac{6}{10}$. ____
10. What is the probability of picking a king out of a pack of playing cards? ____ in ____

11. 9,997, 9,998, 9,999, ____, ____
12. 50% of 90 = ____
13. Write $4\frac{1}{5}$ as an improper fraction. ____
14. What is this 3D shape? ____
15. Is this angle 45° or 90°? ____
16. 8cm 7cm Area = Length × Width = ____ m²
17. -3 -2 -1 0 1 2 3 Circle positive 3.
18. How many days in a leap year? ____
19. 8 + 5 = 20 – a. a = ____
20. ____ + 80 = 145

/20

D · Vocabulary — Wordsearch.

1. There are 5 hundred and _ _ _ _ _ _ weeks in ten years.
2. Round 86 to the nearest ten. _ _ _ _ _ _
3.  This shape is a _ _ _ _ _ _ _ _.
4. The average of 12, 15, 18 is _ _ _ _ _ _ _.
5. 2, 4, 6 and 8 are all _ _ _ _ numbers.

6. What fraction of a cm is 5 mm? A _ _ _ _
7. An _ _ _ _ _ angle is less than a right angle.
8. How many minutes from 4:40 to 6:00? _ _ _ _ _ _
9. 28 is the _ _ _ _ _ _ _ of 7 and 4.
10. The 6th month of the year is _ _ _ _.

o	p	r	o	d	u	c	t	b	p
w	z	i	i	g	n	e	v	e	z
h	d	t	a	c	u	t	e	r	x
f	a	c	y	l	i	n	d	e	r
z	i	l	f	o	q	f	d	y	y
u	z	f	f	y	w	l	d	t	t
p	d	y	t	n	e	w	t	e	h
g	a	y	s	e	m	p	b	n	g
o	e	n	u	j	e	h	q	i	i
x	o	j	k	q	p	n	m	n	e

E · Mental Maths — In your head.

1. Write 3 a.m. in 24 hour time. ____
2. The factors of 16 are ____, ____, ____, ____ and ____.
3. 25% of 100 = ____
4. Write $\frac{15}{2}$ as a mixed number. ____
5. Circle the multiples of 3. 6 11 15
6. $\frac{7}{10}$ = 0· ____
7.  This is the net of a ____.
8. Simplify $\frac{16}{20}$. ____
9. 20% of 80 = ____
10. Write the number sixty point five. ____
11. 7,852. What is the place value of 7? ____

12. Find the average of 11, 13, 17 and 7. ____
13. A ___ B ___ C ___ Which angle is 135°? ____
14. 20% = $\frac{}{100}$ = 0· ____
15. The angles in a rectangle are all ____.
16. 9 x 9 = ____
17. Write the factors of 9. ____ ____ ____
18. 7cm / 4cm Area = Length x Width = ____ cm²
19. Find the perimeter of the shape in question 18. ____
20. -5 -4 -3 -2 -1 0 1 2 3 4 Circle the number negative 2.

/20

F · Puzzle — Problem of the week.

How many rectangles can you see in this pattern?
Remember – a square is a rectangle! ____

G Topic — Area. In your head.

1. What is the area of a rectangle 9 cm long and 7 cm wide? ____

2. What is the area of a square of side 13 cm? ____

3. [18cm / 7cm] Find the area of this rectangle. ____

4. The area of a rectangle is 90 cm². The length is 9 cm. Find the width. ____

5. The area of a square is 49 cm². Find the length of its sides. ____ cm

6. Find the area of this rectangle. [3cm / 4cm] ____

7. A square has a side of 15 cm. What is its perimeter? ____

8. The length of a rectangle is 12 cm and its width is 6 cm. What is its area? ____

9. [11cm / 6cm] [9cm] What is the difference of the area of the rectangle and the area of the square? ____

10. The area of a rectangle is 130 cm². The length is 13 cm. Find the width. ____

11. Find the area of a rectangle length 15 cm and width 6 cm. ____

12. [20cm / 18cm / 16cm / x / 19cm] The perimeter of this pentagon is 85 cm. x = ____ cm

13. The length of a rectangle is 7 cm and the width is 6 cm. Find the perimeter. ____

14. The perimeter of a square is 48 cm. Find the length of a side. ____

15. Find the area of this square. [8cm] ____ cm²

/15

H Topic — Area. Problem solving. In your copy.

1. What does it cost Mary to carpet her sitting room if the room is 8 m long and 6 m wide and carpet is €11·50 per square metre? ____

2. A garage is 6 m long. Its area is 42 m². What is its width? ____

3. The white board in 5th class is 3 m long and 1·5 m wide. It hangs on a wall that is 7 m long and 2·5 m wide.
   (a) What is the area of the white board? ____
   (b) What is the area of the wall? ____
   (c) What is the area of wall not covered by white board? ____

4. Sheila bought 18 square metres of carpet at €36 per square metre. What change did she get out of €800? ____

5. A square tile is 20 cm wide.
   (a) What is the area of the tile? ____
   (b) How many tiles will you need to cover a floor 3 m x 1·2 m? ____

/5

Mental Maths — Beat the clock.

Change the following into minutes. (1 hour = 60 minutes)

1. 1 hour 20 minutes. _____
2. 1 hour 18 minutes. _____
3. 2 hours. _____
4. 1 hour. _____
5. 4 hours 17 minutes. _____
6. 7 hours 40 minutes. _____
7. 12 hours. _____
8. 10 hours 58 minutes. _____
9. 6 hours 5 minutes. _____
10. 3 hours 24 minutes. _____
11. 4 hours 30 minutes. _____
12. 3 hours 15 minutes. _____
13. 2 hours 32 minutes. _____
14. 8 hours 20 minutes. _____
15. 7 hours 9 minutes. _____
16. 5 hours. _____
17. 9 hours 50 minutes. _____
18. 6 hours 39 minutes. _____
19. 10 hours. _____
20. 15 hours. _____

/20

J Code Cracker

Each problem has a letter. Solve the problem and put the letter into the grid to reveal the message! You may use your calculator.

L = $\frac{5}{8}$ of 1,000 = _____
K = $\frac{3}{6}$ of 1,248 = _____
E = $\frac{7}{12}$ of 1,008 = _____
R = $\frac{2}{9}$ of 1,125 = _____

U = $\frac{1}{8}$ of 640 = _____
P = $\frac{4}{7}$ of 952 = _____
O = $\frac{3}{11}$ of 715 = _____
B = $\frac{2}{5}$ of 1,280 = _____

F = $\frac{1}{3}$ of 2,400 = _____
Y = $\frac{7}{10}$ of 1,400 = _____
A = $\frac{3}{13}$ of 871 = _____

625	195	195	624

512	588	800	195	250	588

980	195	80

625	588	201	544

K Puzzle

Arrange the numbers 1 to 9 in the circles so that the sum of the numbers along each side adds up to 20.

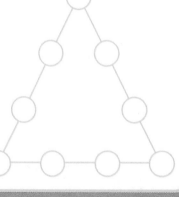

43

A Table Time

Beat the clock.

BAKER STREET

1. (27 ÷ 3) x 5 = ____
2. (80 ÷ 10) x 3 = ____
3. (40 ÷ 5) x 2 = ____
4. (63 ÷ 9) x 7 = ____
5. (60 ÷ 10) x 0 = ____
6. (28 ÷ 7) x 5 = ____
7. (20 ÷ 10) x 4 = ____

8. (9 ÷ 1) x 8 = ____
9. (16 ÷ 4) x 6 = ____
10. (40 ÷ 8) x 9 = ____
11. (30 ÷ 3) x 10 = ____
12. (40 ÷ 4) x 7 = ____
13. (100 ÷ 10) x 9 = ____
14. (36 ÷ 6) x 11 = ____

15. (18 ÷ 9) x 1 = ____
16. (10 ÷ 10) x 10 = ____
17. (27 ÷ 9) x 8 = ____
18. (32 ÷ 8) x 6 = ____
19. (50 ÷ 10) x 12 = ____
20. (81 ÷ 9) x 15 = ____

/20

B Try this

Dividing by 100, 1,000.

 ÷ by 100, 1,000

÷ 100: Move the · left 2 spaces
÷ 1,000: Move the · left 3 spaces

1. 23,400 ÷ 100 = ____
2. 7,950 ÷ 1,000 = ____
3. 237·9 ÷ 1,000 = ____
4. 2,340 ÷ 100 = ____
5. 459·7 ÷ 100 = ____

6. 810 ÷ 1,000 = ____
7. 3,860 ÷ 100 = ____
8. 2,695 ÷ 1,000 = ____
9. 954·3 ÷ 100 = ____
10. 650 ÷ 100 = ____

/10

C Mental Maths

In your head.

1. Write 11 p.m. in 24 hour time. ____
2. 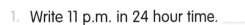 The angles in a regular pentagon are all ____ angles.
3. Write $\frac{3}{100}$ as a decimal. 0· ____
4. The chances of picking a black card from a deck of cards are ____ in ____.
5. The factors of 10 are ____, ____, ____ and ____.
6. Write $\frac{19}{4}$ as a mixed number. ____
7. 10% of 80 = ____
8. 70% = 0·7. True ☐ False ☐
9. Write the number sixty-eight point 5. ____
10. Will this shape tessellate? ____

11. Write $2\frac{7}{10}$ as an improper fraction. ____
12. $\frac{1}{2} < \frac{5}{8}$. True ☐ False ☐
13. -3 -2 -1 0 1 2 3 Circle positive 1.
14. 73,520. What is the value of 7? ____
15. ____ % = $\frac{7}{100}$ = 0·07
16. Write the Roman numeral for 18. ____
17. Round 287 to the nearest 10. ____
18. A decagon has ____ sides.
19. Is 1·01 closer to 1 or 2? ____
20. Write in order from smallest to largest.
0·75 0·25 0·5 ____

/20

D. Vocabulary — Wordsearch.

1. 4, 9, 16, 25 and 36 are all _ _ _ _ _ _ numbers.
2. The eighth month of the year. _ _ _ _ _ _
3. The angles in an equilateral _ _ _ _ _ _ _ _ _ are the same.
4. 100 cm = 1 _ _ _ _ _ _
5. 0·5 of a century is _ _ _ _ _ years.
6. An _ _ _ _ _ _ _ has 8 sides.
7. In shape, a marble is a _ _ _ _ _ _.
8. If Monday is day 1, the third day of the week is _ _ _ _ _ _ _ _ _.
9. The product of 4 and 5 is _ _ _ _ _ _.
10. Multiply one thousand by one thousand = one _ _ _ _ _ _ _.

k	w	y	t	f	i	f	f	z	t
w	e	d	n	e	s	d	a	y	t
f	i	b	r	a	m	l	f	v	r
o	c	t	a	g	o	n	y	s	i
u	e	r	p	d	a	y	g	q	a
m	y	t	n	e	w	t	c	u	n
x	v	m	u	e	l	j	w	a	g
t	n	o	i	l	l	i	m	r	l
d	e	r	e	h	p	s	k	e	e
k	t	s	u	g	u	a	a	y	u

E. Mental Maths — In your head.

1. Write 8 a.m. in 24 hour time. _____
2. Write the number four hundred point seven. _____
3. The probability of picking a red card from a deck of cards is ____ in ____.
4. 10% of 70 = _____
5.  3cm Area = _____ cm² 6cm
6. Find the perimeter of the above shape. _____
7. A ____ B ____ C ____ Which angle is 30°? _____
8. 20 – d = 10 – 4. d = _____
9. Find the average of 7, 9, 12 and 16. _____
10. What is the next prime number after 31? _____
11. A ◯ B △ C ⬡ D ⬡ Which of these shapes will tessellate? _____
12. The factors of 14 are ___, ___, ___ and ___.
13. Is 1·49 closer to 1 or 2? _____
14. $\frac{2}{3} > \frac{5}{6}$. True ☐ False ☐
15. Is 385 evenly divisible by 5? _____
16. How many weeks in a year? _____
17. How many days in 6 school weeks? _____
18. Write the last composite number before 50. _____
19. Find the product of 8 and 50. _____
20. 10% of 50 = _____

/20

F. Puzzle — Problem of the week.

How many of each shape can you find in the triangle?

(a) _____

(b) _____

(c) _____

45

G Topic — Fractions. In your head.

1. Write $\frac{17}{3}$ as a mixed number. ____

2. $\frac{1}{5} = \frac{}{10}$

3. Find $\frac{1}{2}$ of 20 and triple your answer. ____

4. $1 = \frac{}{8}$

5. $\frac{3}{4}$ of 16 minus $\frac{1}{12}$ of 24 = ____

6. $1 - \frac{1}{4} =$ ____

7. $\frac{7}{8} - \frac{1}{2} =$ ____

8. $\frac{3}{5} + \frac{3}{5} = \frac{}{5} = 1\frac{}{5}$

9. $50 - (\frac{3}{8}$ of 64$) =$ ____

10. $(\frac{1}{3} + \frac{1}{3}) - \frac{1}{6} =$ ____ Simplify your answer.

11. $\frac{1}{2} + \frac{2}{6} = \frac{}{6}$

12. $\frac{1}{2} - \frac{3}{10} = \frac{}{10}$

13. $\frac{1}{4} + \frac{11}{12} =$ ____ Write your answer as a mixed number.

14. $\frac{3}{10} + \frac{4}{10} + \frac{5}{10} =$ ____ Write your answer as a mixed number.

15. $1\frac{1}{2} + 2\frac{1}{4} =$ ____

16. $4 \times \frac{1}{6} =$ ____ Write your answer in its lowest terms.

17. $\frac{1}{8} \times 12 =$ ____ Write your answer as a mixed number.

18. $\frac{5}{6} \times 2 =$ ____

19. $3\frac{1}{2} - 1\frac{1}{4} =$ ____

20. $\frac{1}{2} + \frac{1}{4} + \frac{1}{8} = \frac{}{8}$

/20

H Topic — Fractions. Problem solving. In your copy.

1. Pat has €91. He spent $\frac{3}{7}$ of it on a soccer ball.
   (a) How much did he spend? ____
   (b) How much has he left? ____

2. Mary cycled $5\frac{1}{2}$ km on Monday and $4\frac{3}{4}$ km on Tuesday.
   (a) How far did she cycle altogether? ____
   (b) Sam only cycled $6\frac{1}{4}$ km. How much less did he cycle than Mary? ____

3. Áine spent $\frac{1}{4}$ of her money on a games system. She spent €150. How much money had she at first? ____

4. Ciaran wants to buy a bike costing €280. He has saved $\frac{5}{7}$ of the price and his godfather gave him €45 more. How much more does he need to buy the bike? ____

5. (a) Peter had 10 sweets. He lost 6 of them. What fraction did he lose? ____
   (b) Danielle has €50. She spent €40 on a game. What fraction did she spend? ____

6. $\frac{2}{3}$ of a number is 240. What is $\frac{3}{4}$ of it? ____

7. A swimming pool is $\frac{2}{3}$ metre deep at the shallow end. It is 3 times deeper at the other end. How deep is the deeper end?
   ____

/7

I  Mental Maths

Beat the clock.

Change the following to hours and minutes.

1. 120 minutes. _____
2. 132 minutes. _____
3. 60 minutes. _____
4. 75 minutes. _____
5. 480 minutes. _____
6. 105 minutes. _____
7. 93 minutes. _____

8. 560 minutes. _____
9. 126 minutes. _____
10. 10 minutes. _____
11. 180 minutes. _____
12. 68 minutes. _____
13. 210 minutes. _____
14. 240 minutes. _____

15. 258 minutes. _____
16. 29 minutes. _____
17. 290 minutes. _____
18. 300 minutes. _____
19. 15 minutes. _____
20. 365 minutes. _____

/20

J 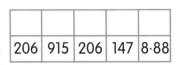 Code Cracker

Each problem has a letter. Solve the problem and put the letter into the grid to reveal the message! You may use your calculator.

E = 61,800 ÷ 300 = _____

V = 3,097 – 2,182 = _____

R = 24·5 x 6 = _____

Y = (5·55 ÷ 5) x 8 = _____

C = 79·58 – 34·48 = _____

A = 95·50 ÷ 5 = _____

I = 9,043 – 8,756 = _____

G = (210 ÷ 3) + (555 ÷ 5) = _____

O = 4,104 ÷ 9 = _____

D = (21,536 + 250) – 21,000 = _____

U = 435 ÷ 29 = _____

N = 1,004 – 793 = _____

S = (216 + 413) – 148 = _____

H = $\frac{5}{8}$ of 552 = _____

L = 25 x 5 = _____

206	915	206	147	8·88

45·1	125	456	15	786

345	19·1	481

19·1

481	287	125	915	206	147

125	287	211	287	211	181

K Puzzle

John likes to eat peas every day. On Monday he ate 20. On Tuesday he ate 30. On Wednesday he ate 50. On Thursday he ate 80. If he continues in this pattern:

(a) How many will he eat on Sunday? _____

(b) How many will he eat in the whole week? _____

A Table Time — Beat the clock.

1. $(15 ÷ 3) + 4 =$ _____
2. $(24 ÷ 2) + 25 =$ _____
3. $(16 ÷ 4) + 12 =$ _____
4. $(21 ÷ 3) + 100 =$ _____
5. $(30 ÷ 5) + 13 =$ _____
6. $(40 ÷ 4) + 50 =$ _____
7. $(36 ÷ 6) + 170 =$ _____
8. $(25 ÷ 5) + 49 =$ _____
9. $(49 ÷ 7) + 19 =$ _____
10. $(54 ÷ 6) + 200 =$ _____
11. $(72 ÷ 8) + 16 =$ _____
12. $(63 ÷ 7) + 72 =$ _____
13. $(81 ÷ 9) + 80 =$ _____
14. $(64 ÷ 8) + 30 =$ _____
15. $(100 ÷ 10) + 10 =$ _____
16. $(45 ÷ 9) + 130 =$ _____
17. $(18 ÷ 0) + 8 =$ _____
18. $(80 ÷ 10) + 35 =$ _____
19. $(40 ÷ 1) + 5 =$ _____
20. $(35 ÷ 7) + 256 =$ _____

/20

B Try this — Revise.

Revision

Multiplying by 10, 100, 1,000
Multiplying decimals
by 10, 100
Dividing by 10, 100, 1,000

1. $7,950 ÷ 10 =$ _____
2. $326·5 ÷ 100 =$ _____
3. $81 × 10 =$ _____
4. $79·5 × 100 =$ _____
5. $86 ÷ 100 =$ _____
6. $38,506 ÷ 1,000 =$ _____
7. $214 × 100 =$ _____
8. $8·5 × 10 =$ _____
9. $386 ÷ 10 =$ _____
10. $412·578 × 1,000 =$ _____
11. $2·4 × 10 =$ _____
12. $3,986·5 ÷ 10 =$ _____
13. $124·68 ÷ 1,000 =$ _____
14. $24 ÷ 10 =$ _____
15. $897 × 1,000 =$ _____

/15

C Mental Maths — In your head.

1. Write 10:00 hours in 12 hour time. _____
2. Round 5·75 to the nearest whole. _____
3. $9,997 + 6 =$ _____
4. $20 ÷ 2 = 2 × f.$ f = _____
5. In 932,200 what is the value of 9? _____
6. The factors of 33 are _____ , _____ , _____ and _____
7. $8,001 - 5 =$ _____
8. Round 265 to the nearest 10. _____
9. 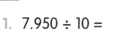 10m 6m Area = _____ m².
10. Write in order from smallest to largest.
    0·6 0·53 0·06 _____

11. $9,992 + 8 =$ _____
12. $38·6 - 17·4 =$ _____
13. $6\% = \frac{}{100} = 0·$
14. Write $\frac{35}{8}$ as a mixed number. _____
15. $\frac{9}{100} =$ _____ %
16. Area of a square with 6 cm sides = _____ cm²
17. ◿ This angle is 45° ☐ 32° ☐ 80° ☐
18. Is $\frac{1}{3}$ equivalent to $\frac{1}{5}$? _____
19. $23·4 + 18·6 =$ _____
20. Is 12 a composite number? _____

/20

D Vocabulary

Wordsearch.

1. The family of numbers that are above and below zero are called d_ _ _ _ _ _ _ _ numbers.

2. Water boils at one _ _ _ _ _ _ _ degrees.

3. Numbers that are less than zero are called _ _g_t_ _ _ numbers.

4. Numbers that are greater than zero are called po_ _ _ _ _ _ numbers.

5. We measure temperature in _ _ _ _ _ _ _.

6. When talking about temperature the c stands for C_ _ _ _ _ _.

c	n	d	e	r	d	n	u	h	b
a	s	e	e	r	g	e	d	c	l
x	r	x	r	m	f	e	k	s	d
l	o	y	g	d	d	v	u	a	e
f	p	o	s	i	t	i	v	e	t
h	d	h	k	l	s	t	s	v	c
u	h	w	j	l	s	a	c	g	e
y	o	s	e	a	x	g	b	e	r
o	r	c	m	o	r	e	q	o	i
d	J	m	c	n	v	n	u	m	d

E Mental Maths

In your head.

1. Write 20:00 hours in 12 hour time. ____
2. Write in order from smallest to largest. 0·3 0·03 0·35 ____ ____ ____
3. How many right angles in a rectangle? ____
4. What 2D shape has 1 edge, 2 faces and 1 vertex? ____
5.  What 2D shape will you see if you cut along the line? ____
6. 3,000 g = ____ kg
7. Circle the multiples of 8. 46 64 48

8. 2,000, 200, 20, ____
9. Is 1·36 closer to 1·30 or 1·40? ____
10. 99,995 + 9 = ____
11. $\frac{1}{4}$ of 120 = ____
12. Write $7\frac{4}{7}$ as an improper fraction. ____
13. $\frac{2}{8} + \frac{3}{8}$ = ____
14. Is this triangle an isosceles triangle? ____
15. Is Z symmetrical? ____

/15

F Puzzle

Problem of the week.

Sudoku

Fill in the boxes so the numbers 1 to 9 appear once in each row, column and small grid.

		4			8	5		7
	7	6		4	3	2		8
6		3			4			
	4	2				1	3	
			8			4		5
4		5	9	2		7	8	
1		8	4			3		

G Topic — Directed Numbers. In your head.

1. Which is colder, ⁻3° C or ⁻5° C? _____

2. Which is warmer, 0° C or ⁻2° C? _____

3. 10, 5, 0, ⁻5, _____, _____, _____

4. 6, 2, ⁻2, _____, _____, _____

5. ⁻25, ⁻20, ⁻15, _____, _____, _____

6. The temperature is ⁻2° C. It rises by 6° C. The new temperature is _____.

7. The temperature is 4° C. It drops by 6° C. The new temperature is _____.

8. What is the difference between 3° C and ⁻2° C? _____

9. What is the freezing point of water, 0° C or 100° C? _____

10. A computer game costs €55. I have saved €28. How much do I need to borrow? _____

11. Circle ⁻2 on the number line. ⁻3 ⁻2 ⁻1 0 1 2 3

12. The temperature dropped from 5° C to ⁻2° C at night. How many degrees did it fall? _____

13. Take the lift from 2 floors below ground level to the 3rd floor above ground level. How many floors do you go up? _____

14. Use the number line to answer these questions. ⁻6 ⁻5 ⁻4 ⁻3 ⁻2 ⁻1 0 1 2 3 4 5 6

    (a) ⁻3 + 4 = _____   (b) 5 − 2 = _____

    (c) 4 + 2 = _____   (d) ⁻5 + 2 = _____

    (e) 3 − 4 = _____

15. The temperature in Dublin is 15° C and is 41° C in Cairo. What is the difference in temperature between the two cities? _____

/15

H Topic — Directed Numbers. Problem solving. In your copy.

1. World Weather

Amsterdam	14°C	London	6°C
Auckland	24°C	Madrid	8°C
Barcelona	13°C	Moscow	⁻5°C
Berlin	2°C	New York	0°C
Cairo	20°C	Stockholm	⁻1°C
Dublin	7°C	Tenerife	18°C
Edinburgh	6°C	Zurich	5°C
Hong Kong	23°C		

(a) Which is the warmest place listed? _____

(b) Which is the coldest place listed? _____

(c) What is the difference in temperature between the warmest and the coldest cities?

_____

(d) If the temperature in each city rose by 5 degrees what would the new temperatures be? _____

(e) If the temperature in each city dropped by 5 degrees what would the new temperatures be? _____

(f) What is the difference in temperature between

   (i) Moscow and New York _____

   (ii) Cairo and Tenerife _____

   (iii) Auckland and Berlin _____

   (iv) Dublin and Stockholm _____

/6

I  Mental Maths

Beat the clock.

Change these fractions to decimals.

1. $1\frac{5}{10} =$ _____
2. $2\frac{6}{100} =$ _____
3. $8\frac{15}{100} =$ _____
4. $3\frac{1}{4} =$ _____
5. $18\frac{4}{5} =$ _____
6. $5\frac{1}{2} =$ _____
7. $17\frac{3}{5} =$ _____

8. $8\frac{1}{3} =$ _____
9. $7\frac{2}{5} =$ _____
10. $56\frac{1}{2} =$ _____
11. $15\frac{28}{100} =$ _____
12. $3\frac{1}{8} =$ _____
13. $11\frac{7}{10} =$ _____
14. $2\frac{1}{5} =$ _____

15. $14\frac{1}{2} =$ _____
16. $23\frac{8}{100} =$ _____
17. $8\frac{45}{1000} =$ _____
18. $4\frac{3}{4} =$ _____
19. $2\frac{1}{10} =$ _____
20. $9\frac{3}{5} =$ _____

/20

J Code Cracker

Across

1. The minutes in $3\frac{3}{4}$ hours
2. $1\cdot89 \times 12$
4. $176\cdot350 - 28\cdot764$
6. 850×3
7. Increase 35,000 by 21%

Down

1. $896 \div 32$
2. $76 + 3{,}174 + 8 + 19{,}204 + 736$
3. $3\cdot685 \times 1{,}000$
5. $c \div 8 = 9$. $c =$ _____
6. $\frac{3}{4}x = 180$. $x =$ _____

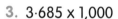

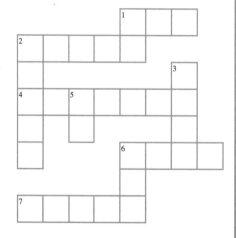

K Puzzle

This block is made of 27 small cubes. The block is painted blue. How many cubes are painted blue:

(a) On 1 side? _____   (b) On 3 sides? _____

(c) On 2 sides? _____   (d) On 0 sides? _____

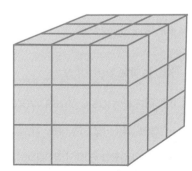

A Table Time — Beat the clock.

1. $(3 \times 1) \div 3$ = ____
2. $(8 \times 8) \times 2$ = ____
3. $(5 \times 3) + 26$ = ____
4. $(5 \times 10) - 40$ = ____
5. $(7 \times 5) \div 7$ = ____
6. $(6 \times 1) - 2$ = ____
7. $(9 \times 7) \times 5$ = ____

8. $(7 \times 3) \div 21$ = ____
9. $(10 \times 9) + 43$ = ____
10. $(8 \times 4) \times 50$ = ____
11. $(11 \times 10) - 36$ = ____
12. $(9 \times 6) + 21$ = ____
13. $(1 \times 11) \div 0$ = ____
14. $(10 \times 7) - 3$ = ____

15. $(2 \times 2) \times 2$ = ____
16. $(4 \times 8) \div 16$ = ____
17. $(3 \times 4) + 25$ = ____
18. $(6 \times 9) \times 3$ = ____
19. $(4 \times 6) - 15$ = ____
20. $(8 \times 10) + 102$ = ____

/20

B Try this — Add to the nearest 10.

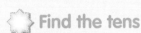

Find the tens

$\overline{16 + 27 + 24}$
$40 + 27 = 67$

1. $15 + 23 + 15$ = ____
2. $21 + 46 + 19$ = ____
3. $53 + 69 + 47$ = ____
4. $25 + 15 + 36$ = ____
5. $8 + 59 + 12$ = ____

6. $19 + 11 + 18$ = ____
7. $35 + 17 + 13$ = ____
8. $83 + 14 + 6$ = ____
9. $17 + 7 + 13$ = ____
10. $27 + 8 + 33$ = ____

/10

C Mental Maths — In your head.

1. Write 9:00 a.m. in 24 hour time. ____
2. $27{\cdot}4 - 13{\cdot}1$ = ____
3. $99{,}999 + 4$ = ____
4. A square has 2 ☐ 4 ☐ lines of symmetry.
5. The chances of a dice landing on an odd number are ____ in ____ .
6. $45\% = 0{\cdot}4$. True ☐ False ☐
7. Is $\frac{2}{4}$ equivalent to $\frac{2}{3}$? ____
8. ◇ This is the net of a ____ .
9. The children in a music class were the following ages: 14, 12, 16, 14, 11, 13, 16, 14. Which age occurred most frequently? ____

10. Area = ____ cm^2

5cm
2cm
3cm
5cm
3cm
2cm

11. Find the perimeter of the shape in question 10. ____ cm
12. Can a square and a triangle tessellate? ____
13. If the diameter of a circle is 6 cm, find the radius. ____
14. Find the average of 175, 300 and 65. ____
15. $4\overline{)4{\cdot}0}$ = ____
16. ▱ This shape is a ____ .
17. $\frac{1}{2} + \frac{2}{6}$ = ____
18. $\frac{1}{2} - \frac{2}{6}$ = ____
19. Round 470 to the nearest hundred. ____
20. Write 11 a.m. in 24 hour time. ____

/20

Vocabulary   Wordsearch.

1. Finding the product of 2 numbers means to
   __ __ __ __ __ __ __.

2. C__ __ __ __ __ __ is the amount of liquid a container can hold.

3. A circular graph is called a p__ __ c__ __ __ __.

4. If something is likely to happen we say it is p__ __ __ __ __ __.

5. There are 1000 millilitres in one __ __ __ __ __.

6. This shape is called a c__ __ __ __ __.

7. The corners of any 3D shape are called its v__ __t__ __ __ __.

8. This sign % means __ __ __ __ __ __ __.

9. One h__ __ __ __ __ % is a whole.

10. 1, 4, 9, 25 and 36 are known as __q__ __ __ __ numbers.

l	y	t	i	c	a	p	a	c	c
i	e	r	a	u	q	s	y	l	u
t	f	a	f	t	s	g	c	m	b
r	s	q	f	x	r	d	f	c	o
e	y	l	p	i	t	l	u	m	i
p	i	e	c	h	a	r	t	n	d
p	r	o	b	a	b	l	e	y	y
z	x	s	e	c	i	t	r	e	v
f	j	g	p	e	r	c	e	n	t
h	u	n	d	r	e	d	s	i	z

 Mental Maths   In your head.

1. Write this time in 24 hour time. ____

2. $\frac{3}{8} + \frac{4}{8} =$ ____

3. $\frac{1}{3}$ of 60 = ____

4. How many faces on a pentagonal prism? ____

5. Write $\frac{3}{100}$ as a decimal. ____

6. 0·6 x 9 = ____

7. Round 795 to the nearest hundred. ____

8. 8, 18, 13, 23, 18, ____, ____

9. In 36·4 the value of 4 is 4 tenths ☐ 4 hundredths ☐.

10. Write in order from largest to smallest. $\frac{1}{2}$ $\frac{5}{8}$ $\frac{3}{4}$ ____ ____ ____

11. An equilateral triangle has 2 ☐ 3 ☐ 6 ☐ lines of symmetry.

12. Write VI as a number. ____

13. $\frac{2}{3}$ of 30 = ____

14. Eileen has the following coins: 10c, 5c, €1, 20c, 20c. Which occurs most frequently? ____

15. Round 470 to the nearest hundred. ____

/15

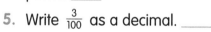 **Puzzle**   Problem of the week.

My watch gains 10 minutes every hour. I set it exactly at midday. Later that evening the clock on the wall says it is 8 p.m. What time does my watch show? ____

G Topic — Decimals. In your head.

1. 0·3, 0·6, 0·9, _____ , _____
2. Write $1\frac{7}{100}$ as a decimal. _____
3. 0·7 of 30 = _____
4. Circle the largest. 6·07 7·60 7·06 6·70
5. 12 is 0·5 of what number? _____
6. Write 0·35 as a fraction in its lowest terms. _____
7. 0·34 = $\frac{}{10}$ + $\frac{}{100}$
8. 0·7 x 3 = _____
9. Round 2·58 to one decimal place. _____
10. 5 x 0·6 = _____
11. Write forty-eight thousandths as a decimal fraction. _____
12. 0·25 of 32 = _____

13. 0·34 x 10 = _____
14. Write $\frac{14}{5}$ as (a) a mixed number _____
    (b) a decimal fraction _____
15. Write in order, starting with the smallest:
    3·2 3·002 3·02 _____ _____ _____
16. Write 0·01 as a fraction. _____
17. 4 – 1·6 = _____
18. Write twenty-eight hundredths as a decimal fraction. _____
19. I have €25. I spend 0·2 of it. What have I left? _____
20. George spent 0·25 of his money. He has €30 left. How much had he at first? _____

/20

H Topic — Decimals. Problem solving. In your copy.

1. Mary bought 6 t-shirts at €16·21 each.
   (a) What was the total bill? _____
   (b) What change did she get from €150? _____
2. 1 bottle holds 1·365 litres of water. How much water do 7 bottles hold? _____
3. Róisin lives 5·304 km from school. She cycles to and from school every day. How far does she cycle in one week? _____
4. George earns €54·55 each day.
   (a) How much does he earn in one working week (5 days)? _____
   (b) How much would he earn in a month? _____

5. 5 children shared a prize of €85·65. How much did each child receive? _____
6. Decorating the church seats for her sister's wedding, Caoimhe made 15 equal ribbons from a roll of ribbon 28·50 m long. How long was each ribbon? _____
7. Gary took 3·79 away from 99·99. He then divided his answer by 26. What was his final answer? _____
8. The area of a rectangle is 991·6 m². Its length is 37 m. What is its width? _____

/8

54

I. Mental Maths

Beat the clock.

Write 15 minutes after:

1. 12:30 = _____
2. 09:45 = _____
3. 11:20 = _____
4. 10:05 = _____
5. 06:50 = _____
6. 04:55 = _____
7. 03:25 = _____

8. 01:05 = _____
9. 02:10 = _____
10. 00:40 = _____

Write 15 minutes before:

11. 11:30 = _____
12. 01:10 = _____
13. 10:55 = _____
14. 09:25 = _____

15. 12:40 = _____
16. 06:35 = _____
17. 05:50 = _____
18. 02:45 = _____
19. 11:20 = _____
20. 08:15 = _____

/20

J. Code Cracker

Each problem has a letter. Solve the problem and put the letter into the grid to reveal the message! You may use your calculator.

T = $7{,}060 \div 10$ = _____

I = $\frac{4}{9}$ of 576 = _____

R = $(67 \times 28) \div 7$ = _____

N = $438 \times$ _____ = 41,610

O = $65 \times$ _____ = 25,805

W = $14{,}835 \div 69$ = _____

F = $24{,}650 \div 25$ = _____

H = $582 \cdot 5 \div 25$ = _____

E = $56{,}841 - 56{,}397$ = _____

S = $216 \cdot 4 \div 4$ = _____

M = $(810 \div 9) \div 5$ = _____

K = $15 \times (13 \times 5)$ = _____

U = $12 \times 7 \times 9$ = _____

706	23·3	444	268	444

256	54·1

95	397

54·1	18	397	975	444

215	256	706	23·3	397	756	706

986	256	268	444

K. Puzzle

The numbers on each side of the hexagon add up to the same number. Fill in the blank circles.

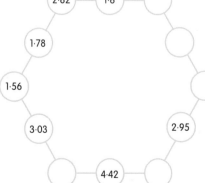

2·82   1·8

1·78

1·56

3·03   2·95

4·42

A Table Time

Beat the clock.

1. (8 + 5) + 29 = ____
2. (3 x 16) – 15 = ____
3. (41 – 16) x 4 = ____
4. (42 ÷ 7) x 8 = ____
5. (6 x 5) + 24 = ____
6. (15 + 15) ÷ 6 = ____
7. (28 ÷ 7) x 15 = ____

8. (61 – 41) x 5 = ____
9. (29 x 5) – 60 = ____
10. (31 + 49) x 2 = ____
11. (56 ÷ 8) + 35= ____
12. (81 – 21) x 4 = ____
13. (2 x 21) + 58 = ____
14. (72 + 6) + 42= ____

15. (72 ÷ 9) + 15 = ____
16. (43 – 15) x 2 = ____
17. (100 ÷ 10) ÷ 10 = ____
18. (5 x 5) x 5 = ____
19. (20 + 20) – 16= ____
20. (100 – 25) x 2= ____

/20

B Try this

Multiplying by 20.

Multiplying by 20

Double the number and x 10

30 x 20 = 32 x 2 x 10

64 x 10 = 640

1. 15 x 20 = ____
2. 75 x 20 = ____
3. 30 x 20 = ____
4. 71 x 20 = ____
5. 61 x 20 = ____

6. 83 x 20 = ____
7. 24 x 20 = ____
8. 94 x 20 = ____
9. 37 x 20 = ____
10. 100 x 20 = ____

/10

C Mental Maths

In your head.

1. Write 2:25 p.m. in 24 hour time. ____
2. $\frac{2}{6} + \frac{1}{3}$ = ____
3. Siobhán earns €150 per day. How much does she earn in 5 days? ____
4. Write $5\frac{2}{9}$ as an improper fraction. ____
5. An isosceles triangle has ____ line of symmetry.
6. $\frac{2}{5}$ of 100 = ____
7. Round 4,826 to the nearest hundred. ____
8. What is the value of 8 in 14·38? ____
9. Which letter is not symmetrical? A S E D
10. 16·85 + 42·37 = ____

11. The diameter of a circle is 12 cm. What is the radius? ____ cm
12. Write in order from largest to smallest.
$\frac{4}{9}$ $\frac{2}{3}$ $\frac{5}{6}$ $\frac{1}{2}$ _____
13. Turn this shape 90° clockwise. ____
14. €50 – €47·60 = ____
15. A pentagon has ____ lines of symmetry.
16. 11 x 0·8 = ____
17. Write the number one before 17,000. ____
18. 43,206 – 10 = ____
19. How many faces on a sphere? ____
20. $\frac{10}{100}$ = 0·____ = ____ %

/20

D Vocabulary — Wordsearch.

1. There are 100 years in a
   _ _ _ _ _ _ _.

2. A ten sided shape is
   called a _ _ _ _ _ _ _.

3. A right angle has
   _ _ _ _ _ _ degrees.

4. The Roman numeral XIX
   stands for
   _ _ _ _ _ _ _ _.

5. The value of 7 in 37,203
   is 7 _ _ _ _ _ _ _ _.

6. 1, 2, 4 and 8 are the
   _ _ _ _ _ _ _ of 8.

7. The corners of 3-
   dimensional shapes are
   called v_ _ _ _ _ _ _.

8. 4, 8, 12, 16 and 20 are all
   _ _lt_ _ _ _ _ of 4.

9. What is the chance word
   for maybe?
   P_ _ _ _ _ _ _

```
n  e  l  b  i  s  s  o  p  c
t  c  s  l  w  h  v  f  o  e
h  a  m  s  r  d  m  z  c  n
o  j  n  o  g  a  c  e  d  t
u  d  t  s  u  q  a  y  c  u
s  f  a  c  t  o  r  s  j  r
a  n  e  e  t  e  n  i  n  y
n  s  e  l  p  i  t  l  u  m
d  s  s  e  c  i  t  r  e  v
s  o  i  s  y  t  e  n  i  n
```

E Mental Maths — In your head.

1. a.m. Write this time in 24 hour
   time. _____

2. $3 \times a = 4 \times 6$. $a =$ _____

3. Write in ascending order. 0·9 0·1 0·01 0·09
   _____ _____ _____ _____

4. $\frac{10}{50} = \frac{}{100}$

5. Angle A = _____°

6. $\frac{1}{4} + \frac{5}{8} =$ _____

7. In 61,300 what is the value of 3? _____

8. $4\overline{)36·4} =$ _____

9. Round 3,606 to the nearest thousand. _____

10. The chances of picking a 10 out of a deck of
    cards are _____ in _____.

11. How many m² of carpet would you need if
    your bedroom was 5 m x 7 m? _____ m²

12. 5·6 x 3 = _____

13. $\frac{2}{5}$ of 60 = _____

14. 20, 13, 24, 17, 28, _____

15. 12 x 12 = _____

16. 48,702 – 8 = _____

17. Simplify $\frac{15}{18}$. _____

18. Write $\frac{24}{5}$ as a mixed number. _____

19. 25% of 60 = _____

20. 35 = half of y. y = _____

/20

F Puzzle — Problem of the week.

Fill in the correct signs (+ or –) to make these number sentences true.

(a) 6 __ 4 __ 2 __ 3 __ 2 __ 5 __ 7 = 1

(b) 5 __ 2 __ 4 __ 8 __ 7 __ 2 __ 1 __ 6 __ 4 = 1

G Topic — Length. In your head.

1. $\frac{1}{2}$ m = ____ cm

2. 750 cm = ____ m ____ cm

3. 2·5 m = ____ cm

4. 3 m – 47 cm = ____ m ____ cm

5. 0·03 m = ____ cm

6. 76 mm = ____ cm ____ mm

7. 4 cm 2 mm + 2$\frac{1}{2}$ cm = ____ cm ____ mm

8. 109 mm = ____ cm ____ mm

9. 4$\frac{9}{10}$ cm = ____ mm

10. $\frac{9}{10}$ m = ____ cm

11. 13$\frac{1}{4}$ m – 9·30 m = ____ m

12. $\frac{1}{5}$ km = ____ m

13. Find the difference between 6$\frac{1}{2}$ m and 4·53 m. ____

14. 3 cm 2 mm x 3 = ____ cm ____ mm

15. $\frac{3}{4}$ km = ____ m

16. A length of material 10·65 m long was divided into 3 equal pieces. How long was each piece? ____

17. 0·750 km = ____ m

18. 9 cm 3 mm – 6 cm 6mm = ____

19. $\frac{3}{4}$ km = ____ m

20. 6,321 m = ____ km

/20

H Topic — Length. Problem solving. In your copy.

1. 3 parcels were stacked on top of each other. The first was 9 cm 8 mm high. The second was 11 cm 8 mm high. The third was 13 cm 6 mm. What was the total height of the 3 boxes? ____

2. Gary cut a piece of string measuring 37·5 cm from a string 85 cm 6 mm long to tie up some sticks. How much string was left? ____

3. Three pencils measure 12·5, 10$\frac{2}{5}$ cm and 13 cm 5 mm. What is their total length? ____

4. A rope measuring 28·40 m long had 2 pieces, 9m 30 cm and 10 m 60 cm, cut off to make skipping ropes. How much was left? ____

5. The shop is 14 m 70 cm high. The bank beside the shop is 17$\frac{1}{4}$ m higher. How high is the taller building? ____

6. When going to visit her cousin Sharon travelled 75 km 360 m altogether. She walked 586 m to the bus stop, travelled 59 km 360 m by bus and the remainder of the journey by car. How far did she travel by car? ____

7. Rachel walked 650 m to the bus stop. She travelled 8 times the distance to get to work. How far did she travel to and from work altogether? ____

/7

I Mental Maths

Beat the clock.

1. $\frac{1}{10} = \frac{}{100} = $ _____ %
2. $\frac{3}{10} = \frac{}{100} = $ _____ %
3. $\frac{6}{10} = \frac{}{100} = $ _____ %
4. $\frac{9}{10} = \frac{}{100} = $ _____ %
5. $\frac{10}{10} = \frac{}{100} = $ _____ %
6. $\frac{1}{4} = \frac{}{100} = $ _____ %
7. $\frac{5}{5} = \frac{}{100} = $ _____ %

8. $\frac{2}{4} = \frac{}{100} = $ _____ %
9. $\frac{3}{5} = \frac{}{100} = $ _____ %
10. $\frac{1}{2} = \frac{}{100} = $ _____ %
11. $\frac{1}{10} + \frac{9}{100} = $ _____ %
12. $\frac{2}{10} + \frac{8}{100} = $ _____ %
13. $\frac{6}{10} + \frac{4}{100} = $ _____ %
14. $\frac{0}{10} + \frac{1}{100} = $ _____ %

15. $\frac{8}{10} + \frac{6}{100} = $ _____ %
16. $\frac{4}{10} + \frac{0}{100} = $ _____ %
17. $\frac{5}{10} + \frac{7}{100} = $ _____ %
18. $\frac{9}{10} + \frac{2}{100} = $ _____ %
19. $\frac{3}{10} + \frac{5}{100} = $ _____ %
20. $\frac{7}{10} + \frac{3}{100} = $ _____ %

/20

J Code Cracker

Each problem has a letter. Solve the problem and put the letter into the grid to reveal the message!
You may use your calculator.

W = 49 + 64 = _____
E = 400 + 177 = _____
T = 81 + 410 = _____
A = 31 x 31 = _____

L = 100 + 4 x 4 = _____
H = 169 + 100 = _____
R = 729 + 121 = _____
S = 196 + (6 x 6) = _____

I = 324 + 247 = _____
Y = (2 x 2) + 64 = _____

William H.
Bloggs
Ways Found

113	269	577	850	577

491	269	577	850	577	232

961

113	571	116	116

491	269	577	850	577	232

961

113	961	68

K Puzzle

Each row and each column is a maths equation.
Use the numbers 1 to 9 to complete each
equation. Each number is used only once.
Remember BOMDAS!

	+		3	+		5	12
x			x			x	
		−			−		-10
+			−			÷	
	+			÷		2	4
29			21			20	

A. Table Time — Beat the clock.

1. (5 x 8) + 16 = ____
2. (10 ÷ 2) x 9 = ____
3. (24 x 10) ÷ 12 = ____
4. (15 + 15) + 16 = ____
5. (36 ÷ 6) x 0 = ____
6. (25 − 10) + 5 = ____
7. (18 ÷ 3) x 14 = ____

8. (8 x 7) + 19 = ____
9. (46 − 24) x 3 = ____
10. (90 ÷ 9) ÷ 2 = ____
11. (15 − 5) x 16 = ____
12. (48 ÷ 6) + 12 = ____
13. (24 + 26) x 2 = ____
14. (17 x 2) + 6 = ____

15. (44 + 20) x 5 = ____
16. (38 − 19) x 2 = ____
17. (2 x 0) + 6 = ____
18. (81 ÷ 9) ÷ 3 = ____
19. (49 + 21) x 3 = ____
20. (65 − 25) + 100 = ____

/20

B. Try this — Multiplying by numbers ending in 0.

x by the number in the tens place, then x 10

40 x 60 = 40 x 6 x 10

240 x 10 = 2,400

1. 70 x 20 = ____
2. 10 x 50 = ____
3. 60 x 30 = ____
4. 20 x 60 = ____
5. 40 x 40 = ____

6. 30 x 70 = ____
7. 50 x 50 = ____
8. 40 x 80 = ____
9. 30 x 60 = ____
10. 50 x 90 = ____

/10

C. Mental Maths — In your head.

1. Write 11:20 p.m. in 24 hour time. ____
2. $\frac{3}{5}$ of 20 = ____
3. 9·68 − 3·34 = ____
4. Six halves of a cake is how many cakes? ____
5.  This is the net of what 3D shape? ____
6. Simplify $\frac{5}{15}$. ____
7. $\frac{3}{10}$ of 80 = ____
8. $\frac{3}{4} − \frac{1}{4}$ = ____
9. $\frac{3}{4} = \frac{}{16}$
10. Write the number five hundred and seventy thousand and seven. ____

11. 11 kg = ____ g
12. $\frac{4}{5}$ + ____ = 1
13. 34·3 ÷ 7 = ____
14. The 4 angles of a quadrilateral add up to 90° ☐ 180° ☐ 360° ☐.
15. A seven-sided shape is called a ____.
16. 0·2 + 0·05 = ____
17. What 2D shape can you see? ____
18. $\frac{3}{4} = \frac{}{12}$
19. Round 9,994 to the nearest hundred. ____
20. Write $\frac{4}{100}$ as a decimal. ____

/20

D  Vocabulary — Wordsearch.

1. 215° = r__ __ __ __ __ angle.
2. kg = k__ __ __ __ __ __ __ __ __
3. Length x Width = __ __ __ __
4. __ __p__ __ __ __ __ is the amount of liquid a container can hold.
5. The Roman numeral XII = __w__ __ __ __

6. An ob__ __ __ __ __ line is a line slanting from the vertical to horizontal.
7. Lines that are always the same distance apart are called __ __ __ __ __ __ __ __ lines.
8. Nine nines are = __ __gh__ __ - __ __ __.

w	e	s	c	e	g	c	o	d	q
a	r	e	a	i	s	c	s	s	l
k	i	l	o	g	r	a	m	m	e
l	e	e	x	h	j	p	b	n	l
t	u	v	e	t	z	a	b	l	l
v	q	l	l	y	h	c	y	v	a
y	i	e	f	o	p	i	u	s	r
s	l	w	e	n	v	t	k	z	a
q	b	t	r	e	e	y	k	o	p
w	o	e	c	b	w	h	a	f	o

E Mental Maths — In your head.

1. Write 5:25 a.m. in 24 hour time. _____
2. 20% of 10 = _____
3. 6·8 x 4 = _____
4. 12 ÷ a = 24 ÷ 8. a = _____
5. 5% = 0·_____
6. $\frac{2}{5}$ of 70 = _____
7. Find the product of 0·6 and 5. _____
8. The radius of a circle is 2·5 cm. The diameter = _____ cm
9. Find the area of a wall 9 m x 4 m. _____ m²
10. $\frac{4}{5} - \frac{2}{10}$ = _____
11. Write 30 hundredths as a decimal. _____

12. Write the 3rd angle of this triangle. x = _____ °
13. $\frac{1}{8}$ + _____ = 1
14. Yvonne earns €140 per day. How much does she earn in 10 days? _____
15. Find the sum of 8·4 and 0·7. _____
16. How many cakes can you make with nine thirds of cake? _____
17. $\frac{17}{50} = \frac{}{100}$
18. Write 17:40 hours in 12 hour time. _____
19. 55 m = _____ cm
20. 7·5 kg = _____ g

 /20

F Puzzle

Problem of the week.

Complete the magic squares.

5		6	
2	15		
9	4		
14	3	13	

1		13	
			7
		1	9
15	10	3	6

G   Topic   3D Shapes. In your head.

1. A cube as ____ faces.
2. Name this shape. ____
3. This is the net for which 3D shape? ____
4. Is this a regular or irregular pentagon? ____
5. What shape is a tin of soup? ____
6. Name this shape. ____
7. A cone has ____ faces.
8. A cylinder has ____ vertices.
9. A cuboid has ____ vertices.

10. This is the net for which 3D shape? ____
11. What two 3D parts make up a pencil? ____ and ____
12. Name this 3D shape. ____
13. A square-based pyramid has ____ edges.
14. What is the perimeter of a square of side 9 m? ____
15. This is the net for which 3D shape? ____

/15

H   Topic   3D Shapes. Problem solving. In your copy.

1. Fill in this grid.

3D shape	Name	No of faces	No of vertices	No of edges	No of edges meeting at each vertex

1. Mental Maths — Beat the clock.

What change would I get from €5 if I spent these amounts of money?

1. €3·75 _____
2. €2·30 _____
3. €4·90 _____
4. €2·92 _____
5. €1·15 _____
6. €4·55 _____
7. €4·20 _____

8. €2·07 _____
9. €1·95 _____
10. €0·85 _____
11. €4·08 _____
12. €1·64 _____
13. €3·18 _____
14. €5·00 _____

15. €2·16 _____
16. €3·41 _____
17. €1·05 _____
18. €4·98 _____
19. €0·50 _____
20. €2·64 _____

/20

J. Code Cracker

Each problem has a letter. Solve the problem and put the letter into the grid to reveal the message! You may use your calculator.

A = 40 x 20 = _____
R = 87 x 10 = _____
W = 84 x 9 = _____
I = (250 ÷ 5) x 12 = _____
M = 45 x 8 = _____

L = 15 x 19 = _____
U = 47 x 18 = _____
H = (125 x 15) – 1,221 = _____
D = 13 x 13 = _____
O = $\frac{4}{5}$ of 365 = _____

N = $\frac{3}{8}$ of 1,640 = _____
G = 25 x 25 = _____
C = (1,226 – 1,023) x 3 = _____
T = 74 x (9 ÷ 3) = _____
S = 78 x (48 ÷ 6) = _____

800

169	870	292	756	615	600	615	625

360	800	615

756	600	285	285

609	285	846	222	609	654

800	222

800

624	222	870	800	756

K. Puzzle

The zeros have been removed from these sums. Put them back to make the problems make sense. The first one has been done for you.

	35			35
	+17	→		+107
	142 X			142

	42			
	+14	→		
	146 X			146

	14			
	+18	→		
	194 X			194

A Table Time — Beat the clock.

1. (6 x 5) x 2 = ____
2. (21 ÷ 7) + 34 = ____
3. (8 x 3) – 17 = ____
4. (15 – 4) + 12 = ____
5. (17 x 3) + 9 = ____
6. (54 ÷ 6) ÷ 3 = ____
7. (17 + 17) ÷ 2 = ____

8. (12 x 12) x 1 = ____
9. (9 ÷ 3) x 8 = ____
10. (5 x 5) ÷ 1 = ____
11. (11 x 11) x 2 = ____
12. (81 ÷ 9) x 7 = ____
13. (7 x 7) + 11 = ____
14. (49 – 6) + 27 = ____

15. (8 x 8) + 16 = ____
16. (24 ÷ 2) ÷ 3 = ____
17. (6 x 6) x 5 = ____
18. (18 + 18) + 18 = ____
19. (9 x 9) + 19 = ____
20. (42 ÷ 6) + 84 = ____

/20

B Try this — BOMDAS.

BOMDAS

Brackets, Of, Multiplication,
Division, Addition,
Subtraction

Solve what is inside the brackets first, then 'of' followed by multiplication, then division, then addition and finally subtraction.

1. (40 – 10) + 30 = ____
2. (16 ÷ 4) + 3 = ____
3. (50 + 10) x 2 = ____
4. 8 + 18 ÷ 6 = ____
5. 12 + 12 ÷ 2 = ____

6. (8 + 16) ÷ 12 = ____
7. (72 ÷ 9) + 4 = ____
8. (63 ÷ 7) x 4 = ____
9. 3 + 8 x 5 = ____
10. 6 x 21 ÷ 7 = ____

/10

C Mental Maths — In your head.

1. Write 5:20 a.m. in 24 hour time. ____
2. How many hours are there between 9 a.m. and 7 p.m.? ____
3. 25% of a dozen = ____
4. 75% of a year = ____
5. 29 is $\frac{1}{2}$ of a. a = ____
6. 0·03 > 0·3. True ☐ False ☐
7. What is the value of 3 in 364,012? ____
8.  A = ____ °
9. 99,995 + 8 = ____
10. 0·02 + 0·5 = ____

11. $\frac{3}{4}$ of 120 = ____
12. Write the number directly after 4,909. ____
13. Write the next prime number after 11. ____
14. (36 ÷ 4) – 5 = ____
15. 7 + 9 + 11 = ____
16. 2 x 2 x 2 = ____
17. Circle the unit you would use to measure a pen. cm m
18. $\frac{9}{12} - \frac{1}{2}$ = ____
19. 6 x 3·85 = ____
20. ⟋ This angle is > 90° ☐, < 90° ☐, = 90° ☐.

/20

D Vocabulary

1. A shape with four equal sides and angles.
   _ _ _ _ _ _

2. Seventy-five plus _ _ _ _ _ _ _ is ninety.

3. Half a circle.
   _ _ _ _ _ _ _ _ _ _

4. 180° = a
   _ _ _ _ _ _ _ _ angle

5. An eight sided shape is called an _ _ _ _ _ _ _ _.

6. A _ _ _ _ _ _ _ _ is a square pushed out of shape.

7. Eighty-one divided by nine. _ _ _ _

8. Shapes that fit perfectly together are said to t_ _ _ _ _ _ _ _ _.

9. 180 minutes = _ _ _ _ _ hours

10. The third month of the year. _ _ _ _ _

c	e	y	e	m	a	r	c	h	u
s	e	m	i	c	i	r	c	l	e
t	e	s	s	e	l	l	a	t	e
h	l	n	l	e	k	s	d	h	d
r	n	o	g	a	t	c	o	g	i
e	n	i	n	e	e	t	f	i	f
e	j	t	p	y	l	a	n	a	g
s	q	u	a	r	e	w	m	r	y
q	a	v	v	p	a	c	s	t	c
f	s	u	b	m	o	h	r	s	s

E Mental Maths

In your head.

1. Write 12:10 a.m. in 24 hour time. _____

2. $0·06 + 0·6 =$ _____

3. ◇ This is the net of a _____.

4. Four quarters of an orange is how many oranges? _____

5. $\frac{2}{5} = \frac{}{10}$

6. $82·62 - 31·58 =$ _____

7. The value of 3 in 58·932 is 3 tenths ☐ hundredths ☐ thousandths ☐.

8. $7 \times 0·4 =$ _____

9. Round 7,136 to the nearest thousand. _____

10. What change would I get from €20 if I spend €15·45? _____

11. $0·2 =$ _____ %

12. ⬡ What shape is this? _____

13. The chances of being born on a Friday are _____ in _____.

14. 2cm / 2cm / 2cm / 2cm / 4cm / 4cm What is the area of this shape? _____

15. What is the perimeter of the shape in question 15? _____

/15

F Puzzle

Problem of the week.

John was asked to pick a number, then to triple it, next to halve the answer and then he subtracted 15 from it. His answer was 21. What was the number he chose?
Hint: Work backwards.

21

G Topic

Number Sequences. In your head.

1. 1, 3, 5, ____, ____

2. 9, 17, 25, ____, ____, ____

3. $\frac{1}{4}$, $\frac{1}{5}$, ____, $\frac{1}{7}$, ____, ____

4. 1·2, 1·1, ____, ____, 0·8, ____

5. Odd number x odd number = ____ number

6. What is the next multiple of 6 after 72? ____

7. Write the first 4 multiples of 4. ___ ___ ___ ___

8. Write the first 4 multiples of 25. ____ ____
    ____ ____

9. List all the factors of 16. ___ ___ ___ ___ ___

10. Write the 3 prime numbers just before 60.
    ____ ____ ____

11. List the composite numbers between 24 and
    30. ____ ____ ____ ____ ____ ____

12. List the multiples of 3 between 17 and 30.
    ____ ____ ____ ____

13. Is 6 a factor of 58? ____

14. Is 33 a rectangular number? ____

15. List the even numbers between 57 and 67.
    ____ ____ ____ ____ ____

16. What is the sum of the composite numbers
    between 10 and 17? ____

17. 6, 7, 10, 15, ____, ____, ____

18. Write the first 5 even numbers. ____ ____
    ____ ____ ____

19. What is the last prime number before 100?
    ____

20. Is 7 a factor of 91? ____

/20

H Topic

**Number Sequences. Problem solving.
In your copy.**

1. (a) Write all the even numbers between
    31 and 47. ____
    (b) Write all the prime numbers between
    31 and 47. ____
    (c) Write all the odd numbers between
    31 and 47. ____

2. (a) 1, 5, 9, 13, ____, ____
    (b) 3, 6, 12, 24, ____, ____
    (c) 1, 3, 6, 10, ____, ____
    (d) 64, 32, 16, 8, ____, ____
    (e) 25, 24, 22, 19, ____, ____

3. (a) Circle the composite numbers.
    11 15 25 33 41 51 63 79 81 83
    (b) Circle the prime numbers.
    21 23 27 29 33 37 41 43 45 49

4. Circle the rectangular numbers and write
    the factors.
    14 19 27 32 35 40 41 47 48

5. (a) Write the next even number after 40. ____
    (b) Write the next prime number after 60.
    ____
    (c) Write the last rectangular number before
    80. ____
    (d) Write the last composite number before
    70. ____
    (e) Write the next multiple of 4 after 68. ____

/5

I. Mental Maths

Beat the clock.

Show these fractions in their lowest terms.

1. $\frac{4}{10}$ = _____

2. $\frac{5}{20}$ = _____

3. $\frac{6}{8}$ = _____

4. $\frac{7}{9}$ = _____

5. $\frac{2}{4}$ = _____

6. $\frac{22}{36}$ = _____

7. $\frac{3}{9}$ = _____

8. $\frac{12}{36}$ = _____

9. $\frac{4}{8}$ = _____

10. $\frac{14}{18}$ = _____

11. $\frac{5}{10}$ = _____

12. $\frac{4}{16}$ = _____

13. $\frac{6}{9}$ = _____

14. $\frac{3}{6}$ = _____

15. $\frac{8}{24}$ = _____

16. $\frac{3}{12}$ = _____

17. $\frac{19}{21}$ = _____

18. $\frac{11}{12}$ = _____

19. $\frac{16}{20}$ = _____

20. $\frac{46}{67}$ = _____

/20

J. Code Cracker

Each problem has a letter. Solve the problem and put the letter into the grid to reveal the message!
You may use your calculator.

T = 4,786 – 3,987 = _____

M = 3,501 – 2,765 = _____

N = 3,478 – 2,545 = _____

C = (8,749 – 4,877) ÷ 4 = _____

S = 7,987 – 7,488 = _____

I = 360 ÷ 5 = _____

H = (5·6 x 7·5) x 10 = _____

B = 5,412 – 4,511 = _____

O = 97 x (8 ÷ 2) = _____

A = 14 x 8 = _____

Y = 3,874 – 3,258 = _____

K = 24 x 9 = _____

P = 15 x 15 = _____

L = 3,972 ÷ 4 = _____

E = $\frac{3}{8}$ of 1,472 = _____

R = 148 ÷ 2 = _____

799	388	388

736	112	933	616

968	388	388	216	499

499	225	388	72	993

799	420	552

901	74	388	799	420

K. Puzzle

A zoo has several ostriches and several giraffes.
Between them they have 30 eyes and 44 legs.
How many of each does the zoo have?

A Table Time

Beat the clock.

1. (25 x 4) x 3 = ____
2. (16 ÷ 4) + 26 = ____
3. (81 ÷ 9) – 3 = ____
4. (72 ÷ 6) x 5 = ____
5. (10 x 4) ÷ 2 = ____
6. (18 x 5) x 6 = ____
7. (8 + 3) + 24 = ____

8. (16 x 5) ÷ 8 = ____
9. (81 – 51) x 5 = ____
10. (13 x 3) + 17 = ____
11. (50 x 21) ÷ 10 = ____
12. (14 x 5) – 17 = ____
13. (18 + 14) + 8 = ____
14. (32 – 15) ÷ 1 = ____

15. (8 x 6) x 2 = ____
16. (36 + 19) + 5 = ____
17. (16 x 4) – 7 = ____
18. (22 x 5) – 10 = ____
19. (24 x 4) ÷ 8 = ____
20. (7 x 5) x 2 = ____

/20

B Try this

Using 100 to multiply by 25.

 x by 25

x by 100 then ÷ by 4

36 x 25

36 x 100 = 3600 ÷ 4 = 900

1. 18 x 25 = ____
2. 43 x 25 = ____
3. 17 x 25 = ____
4. 54 x 25 = ____
5. 24 x 25 = ____

6. 12 x 25 = ____
7. 38 x 25 = ____
8. 59 x 25 = ____
9. 90 x 25 = ____
10. 86 x 25 = ____

/10

C Mental Maths

In your head.

1. Write 11:24 p.m. in 24 hour time. ____
2. A tetrahedron has ____ vertices.
3. a x a = 64. a = ____
4. Write the number 1 before 10,000. ____
5. The radius of a circle is 5·5 cm. Find the diameter. ____ cm
6. Share 60 apples between 10 people. ____
7. Write a symmetrical letter. ____
8. $\frac{3}{4} - \frac{3}{8}$ = ____
9. 6·25 x 5 = ____
10. Circle the net that will make a cube.

11. 3 x 3 x 3 = ____
12. List the composite numbers between 70 and 80. ____
13. 399,964 – 8 = ____
14. 10 x 10 > 111. True ☐ False ☐
15. 0·04 + 0·05 = ____
16. The Roman numeral VIII stands for ____.
17. 12 x 12 = ____
18. A cube has ____ vertices.
19. $\frac{3}{5}$ = $\frac{}{10}$
20. The chances of picking a king or a queen from a pack of cards are ____ in ____.

/20

D Vocabulary — Wordsearch.

1. 5 is a _ _ _ _ _ _ of 20.
2. There are _ _ _ _ sides on a pentagon.
3. A _ _ _ _ _ _ _ _ triangle has all different sides and angles.
4. > = _ _ _ _ _ _ _ than
5. = means _ _ _ _ _ _

6. The 1900s are the _ _ _ _ _ _ _ _ _ century.
7. 20 is a _ _ _ _ _ _ _ _ of 5.
8. < = _ _ _ _ than
9. The twelfth month of the year is _ _ _ _ _ _ _ _.
10. Area = _ _ _ _ _ _ x width.

d	e	c	e	m	b	e	r	l	w
e	g	t	h	u	r	t	c	e	l
q	m	d	t	e	o	w	y	s	e
u	u	m	g	k	t	e	d	s	n
a	l	w	i	s	c	n	a	i	g
l	t	g	r	e	a	t	e	r	t
s	i	v	m	z	f	i	v	e	h
s	p	s	c	a	l	e	n	e	p
x	l	o	a	e	r	t	c	a	u
q	e	e	e	c	d	h	k	z	y

E Mental Maths — In your head.

1. Write 1:45 p.m. in 24 hour time. _____
2. 39·48 – 29·57 = _____
3. What is the place value of 6 in 41,603? _____
4. Write the number 1 before 17,043. _____
5. 8 x 0·6 = _____
6. What change would I get from €50 if I spend €29·38? _____
7. 10% of 650 = _____
8. Write the number 4 before 17,043. _____
9. 8 eighths of pizza is how many pizzas? _____
10. This timetable shows flight times from Dublin to Heathrow.

Flight	AA16	AA17	AA18	AA19
Dep. Dublin	06:40	11:35	16:05	21:00
Arr. Heathrow	07:55	12:50	17:20	22:15

(a) How long does each flight take to complete? _____
(b) Which flight takes off at 16:05? _____
(c) Which flight lands at 12:50? _____
(d) You need to be in Heathrow by 9 p.m. Which flight should you take? _____

/10

F Puzzle — Problem of the week.

A man has 50 red and 50 black socks in a drawer. He is blindfolded. What is the least number of socks he must pick from the drawer to get a pair the same colour? _____

G   Topic   Chance. In your head.

1. When tossing a coin, what are the two possible outcomes? _____

2. How many possible outcomes are there when throwing a dice? _____

3. Which is certain? The sun will shine today ☐ It will rain today ☐ It will get dark tonight ☐

4. Which is probable? I will watch TV today ☐ I will go to work today ☐ I will wash the car today ☐

5. Which is impossible? I will eat a burger ☐ I will eat an egg ☐ I will eat a chair ☐

6. What are the chances we will all be asleep by 2:00 a.m.? Impossible ☐ probable ☐ certain ☐

7. There are 5 bananas, 3 apples and 2 pears in a bowl. What are the chances of picking a banana? _____ in _____

8. When rolling a dice, what are the chances of getting an even number? _____ in _____

9. What are the chances a dinosaur will walk into your house? Probable ☐ possible ☐ impossible ☐

10. What are the chances of picking a black card from a deck of cards? _____ in_____

11. What are the chances of picking the 2 of hearts from a deck of cards? _____ in_____

12. What are the chances that you were born on a Monday? _____ in _____

13. There are 3 green, 5 blue, 4 red and 6 black pens in a pencil case. What are the chances of picking a green pen? _____ in _____

14. What are the chances of picking a blue or green pen from the same pencil case? _____ in _____

15. In an art class there are 12 girls and 9 boys. What are the chances of picking a boy? _____ in _____

/15

H   Topic   Chance. Problem solving. In your copy.

1. The sun was beaming in a blue sky one bright summer's day. Sharon and Cathal went for a cycle up the mountains to Glenbarrow, Co. Laois. They wanted to have a picnic beside the waterfall. The waterfall was situated in the middle of a pine forest. Read the statements and decide if they are probable, improbable, definite or impossible.

(a) It will rain on their picnic. _____

(b) Sharon and Cathal are in a county in Munster. _____

(c) They will meet a farmer along the way. _____

(d) They will see two or three trees near them. _____

(e) They will see a squirrel. _____

(f) Fungie the dolphin will be swimming below the waterfall. _____

(g) Sharon or Cathal will get wet. _____

(h) They will buy a drink at the supermarket nearby. _____

(i) They will get sunburnt. _____

(j) They will be annoyed by flies. _____

/10

70

Beat the clock.

1. 17, 18, 19, ____ , ____
2. 60, 120, 180, ____ , ____
3. 20, 25, 30 ____ , ____
4. 4, 8, 12, ____ , ____
5. 29, 36, 43, ____ , ____
6. 32, 36, 40, ____ , ____
7. 350, 415, 480, ____ , ____

8. 28, 31, 34, ____ , ____
9. 43, 58, 73, ____ , ____
10. 81, 90, 99, ____ , ____
11. 37, 62, 87, ____ , ____
12. 3, 5, 7, ____ , ____
13. 14, 20, 26, ____ , ____
14. 13, 17, 21, ____ , ____

15. 400, 500, 600, ____ , ____
16. 77, 88, 99, ____ , ____
17. 28, 38, 48, ____ , ____
18. 60, 63, 66, ____ , ____
19. 44, 64, 84, ____ , ____
20. 30, 40, 50, ____ , ____

/20

J Code Cracker

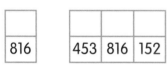

Each problem has a letter. Solve the problem and put the letter into the grid to reveal the message!
You may use your calculator.

A $= \frac{4}{5}$ of 1,020 = ____

D $= \frac{4}{10}$ of 380 = ____

O $= \frac{9}{17}$ of 1,190 = ____

K $= \frac{1}{5}$ of 685 = ____

N $= \frac{11}{13}$ of 1,170 = ____

E $= \frac{3}{4}$ of 1,248 = ____

H $= \frac{1}{6}$ of 660 = ____

T $= \frac{13}{17}$ of 1,088 = ____

B $= \frac{3}{4}$ of 604 = ____

W $= \frac{8}{10}$ of 720 = ____

R $= \frac{5}{16}$ of 480 = ____

M $= \frac{8}{40}$ of 4,000 = ____

L $= \frac{1}{4}$ of 240 = ____

S $= \frac{10}{10}$ of 400 = ____

I $= \frac{7}{8}$ of 648 = ____

816

453	816	152

576	630	150	137	800	816	990

453	60	816	800	936	400

110	567	400

832	630	630	60	400

K Puzzle

Four children are sitting at a table. In order from youngest to oldest, they are George, Katie, Rachel and Cillian. The younger girl is on Cillian's left, and opposite her is her sister. George and Cillian both wanted to sit near the window so they tossed a coin and George won.

Name the children seated at the table.

A Table Time — Beat the clock.

1. $(50 \times 7) \times 3$ = ____
2. $(8 + 3) \div 11$ = ____
3. $(21 \times 6) - 50$ = ____
4. $(71 + 5) + 18$ = ____
5. $(6 \times 8) \div 4$ = ____
6. $(7 \times 9) \times 2$ = ____
7. $(7 \times 7) + 24$ = ____

8. $(30 \times 3) - 48$ = ____
9. $(9 \times 9) \times 3$ = ____
10. $(10 \times 12) \div 6$ = ____
11. $(10 \times 10) - 84$ = ____
12. $(37 + 37) + 24$ = ____
13. $(4 \times 15) \div 2$ = ____
14. $(6 \times 9) \times 2$ = ____

15. $(24 + 6) + 20$ = ____
16. $(20 \times 8) - 60$ = ____
17. $(8 \times 7) \times 9$ = ____
18. $(25 \times 5) \div 5$ = ____
19. $(17 - 9) - 2$ = ____
20. $(12 \times 2) + 26$ = ____

/20

B Try this — Revision.

Revision

1. 180×50 = ____
2. $16 + 14 + 32$ = ____
3. 400×60 = ____
4. $81 + (15 \div 5)$ = ____
5. 16×25 = ____
6. $37 + 18 + 23$ = ____
7. 18×25 = ____
8. $17 + 21 \div 7$ = ____

9. 600×70 = ____
10. $15 + 29 + 61$ = ____
11. 900×80 = ____
12. $96 + 24 + 26$ = ____
13. $(72 \div 9) + 4$ = ____
14. 60×25 = ____
15. $3 + 10 \div 2$ = ____

/15

C Mental Maths — In your head.

1. 2 cm = ____ mm
2. $5 \cdot 302 + 10 \cdot 598 + 7 \cdot 325$ = ____
3. Will a hexagon and a square tessellate? ____
4. Which 3D shape has 2 triangular and 3 rectangular faces? ____
5. 1×1 = ____
6. Write $\frac{9}{2}$ as a mixed number. ____
7. $20\% = \frac{1}{4}$. True ☐ False ☐
8. $\frac{9}{10} - \frac{2}{5}$ = ____
9. 50% of €50 = ____
10. $5 \cdot 0 \times 0 \cdot 05$ = ____

11. $\frac{3}{4} + \frac{2}{4}$ = ____ Write your answer as a mixed number.
12. $\frac{71}{100}$ = ____ %
13. ☐ Turn this shape 90° anticlockwise. ____
14. Write the Roman numeral for 25. ____
15. Find the diameter of a circle whose radius is 3·1 cm. ____
16. Is 344 divisible by 9 with no remainder? ____
17. Ⓒ Turn this shape 180° anticlockwise. ____
18. $0 \cdot 06 + 4 + 0 \cdot 3$ = ____
19. 9×9 = ____
20. $0 \cdot 55 \times 3$ = ____

/20

D Vocabulary

Wordsearch.

1. How many €5 in €100?

   _ _ _ _ _ _

2. Walls are

   _ _ _ _ _ _ _ _.

3. 20 minutes is one

   _ _ _ _ _ of an hour.

4. Fourteen multiplied by

   five = _ _ _ _ _ _ _

5. Reduce means to make

   s_ _ _ _ _

6. Reduce €50 by €10 =

   _ _ _ _ _ euro

7. A nine sided shape is

   called a

   _ _ _ _ _ _ _.

8. An _ _ _ _ _ _ _ _ _

   triangle has 2 sides the

   same length.

9. The seventh month of the

   year is _ _ _ _.

a	l	n	o	g	a	n	o	n	h
l	c	t	q	a	l	s	h	h	w
e	m	w	f	n	a	c	q	r	t
l	s	e	l	e	c	s	o	s	i
l	l	n	t	h	i	r	d	j	f
a	x	t	u	n	t	w	s	u	o
r	v	y	o	q	r	x	r	l	r
a	q	s	e	v	e	n	t	y	t
p	c	w	x	h	v	d	n	n	y
v	r	e	l	l	a	m	s	b	n

E Mental Maths

In your head.

1. 4,321 m = ____ km
2. Round 3·69 to nearest tenth. ____
3. 10 x a = 100. a = ____
4. $\frac{11}{12} - \frac{5}{6} =$ ____
5. There are 6 apples in each bag. There are 9 bags. How many apples altogether? ____
6. What is the cost of 2 litres of water at 80c per 500 ml? ____
7. $\frac{1}{4} + \frac{3}{6} =$ ____
8. What is the place value of 6 in 3·56? ____
9. 700 x 7 = ____
10. Write the number 2 more than 89,999. ____
11. Write $\frac{17}{7}$ as a mixed number. ____
12. Circle the larger. 13,030 13,300
13. 8 x 8 = ____
14. Write the next prime number after 23. ____
15. Find the area of a square with 7 cm sides. ____

/15

F Puzzle

Problem of the week.

Sudoku

Fill in the boxes so the numbers 1 to 9 appear once in each row, column and small grid.

7	9					3		
					6	9		
8				3			7	6
					5			2
		5	4	1	8	7		
4			7					
6	1			9				8
		2	3					
		9					5	4

G Topic — Percentages. In your head.

1. $\frac{7}{10}$ = _____ %

2. $\frac{1}{4}$ = $\frac{25}{100}$ = _____ %

3. Write 0·08 as a percentage. _____%

4. 20% of 450 = _____

5. $\frac{7}{20}$ = $\frac{}{100}$ = _____ %

6. 0·2 = $\frac{}{10}$ = $\frac{}{100}$ = _____%

7. I spent 25% of €88. How much have I left? _____

8. Add 75% of 48 and 50% of 40. _____

9. $\frac{4}{5}$ = _____%

10. 0·875 = _____ %

11. I spent 30% of my money on a CD and 55% on a pair of jeans. What percentage do I have left? _____

12. Joe did $\frac{2}{3}$ of his homework before tea. What percentage did he do after tea? _____

13. Find the sum of 40% of 60 and 30% of 90. _____

14. Put in the correct sign: <, > or =.
    87% _____ $\frac{7}{10}$ + $\frac{8}{100}$

15. 100% = $\frac{}{100}$

/15

H Topic — Percentages. Problem solving. In your copy.

1. Complete this chart.

Fraction	$\frac{1}{2}$			$\frac{1}{5}$				$\frac{1}{8}$		$\frac{17}{100}$
%			30%		$33\frac{1}{3}$%		15%		31%	
Decimal		0·75				0·70				

2. Mary read 36% of her book on Monday, 28% on Tuesday and the remainder on Wednesday. What percentage did she read on Wednesday? _____

3. 40% of the people in a town of population 7,560 owned a car. How many people owned a car? _____

4. (a) There were 40 questions in Sean's maths test. If he got 35 right, what percentage did he get right? _____
   (b) There are 25 players in a hurling club. If 18 of them travelled to a match by bus, what percentage travelled on the bus? _____

5. Alice set out on a journey of 360 km. When she had covered 80% of her journey how much further had she to go? _____

6. Jim won €3,760. Sharon won 30% of that.
   (a) How much did Sharon win? _____
   (b) How much did they win between them? _____

7. A farmer sold one horse for €1,285. He got 20% more for the second horse.
   (a) How much did he get for the second horse? _____
   (b) How much did he get altogether? _____

/7

I. Mental Maths

Beat the clock.

Put in the correct sign: >, <, or =.

1. 31 + 16 _____ 40
2. 9 x 4 _____ 36
3. 30 + 10 _____ 5 x 6
4. 7 x 5 _____ 13
5. 18 + 18 _____ 38
6. 81 ÷ 9 _____ 5 + 5
7. 23 + 6 _____ 31

8. 9 x 6 _____ 6 + 9
9. 48 ÷ 8 _____ 24 ÷ 3
10. 8 x 5 _____ 5 x 8
11. 41 + 3 _____ 12 x 3
12. 31 + 15 _____ 7 x 7
13. 8 ÷ 2 _____ 4 ÷ 1
14. 15 x 4 _____ 61

15. 19 + 19 _____ 50 – 22
16. 20 x 5 _____ 100 – 5
17. 16 + 16 _____ 64 ÷ 2
18. 16 + 13 _____ 21 + 2
19. 26 + 28 _____ 28 + 26
20. 80 – 17 _____ 36 + 20

/20

J. Code Cracker

Across

1. The months in a century
2. 15 x 15 x 6
3. The sum of the even numbers between 40 and 54
5. 80% of 25,000
6. The 9th multiple of 8
7. The largest number possible made from 3, 0, 9, 2 and 5

Down

1. 10 x 10 x 10 x 10 x 10
3. 5% of 4,000
4. $\left(\frac{3}{4} \text{ of } 22{\cdot}52\right) + \left(31{\cdot}38 \div 6\right)$
5. 39 + 876 + 8,675 + 9 + 15,436

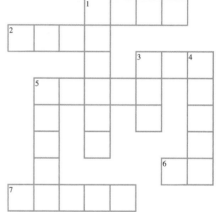

K. Puzzle

A pole is stuck into a hole in the ground. $\frac{1}{2}$ the length of the pole is in the clay, $\frac{1}{3}$ is covered by water and the remaining 8 metres is above the water. How long is the pole? _____

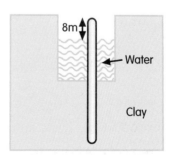

8m — Water — Clay

A Table Time — Beat the clock.

1. (81 x 5) x 6 = ____
2. (6 x 8) – 8 = ____
3. (7 x 4) ÷ 2 = ____
4. (5 x 8) ÷ 8 = ____
5. (24 x 2) x 2 = ____
6. (6 x 10) + 80 = ____
7. (16 ÷ 8) x 10 = ____

8. (7 x 9) + 7 = ____
9. (14 ÷ 7) x 14 = ____
10. (8 x 2) – 3 = ____
11. (6 ÷ 2) x 5 = ____
12. (3 x 6) – 10 = ____
13. (66 ÷ 11) + 17 = ____
14. (7 x 1) x 3 = ____

15. (12 x 3) ÷ 9 = ____
16. (16 ÷ 4) + 18 = ____
17. (12 ÷ 4) – 1 = ____
18. (8 ÷ 8) x 0 = ____
19. (8 x 6) ÷ 4 = ____
20. (81 ÷ 9) + 10 = ____

/20

B Try this — Subtraction.

Subtraction

249 – 68 = 249 – 70 + 2

181

1. 93 – 54 = ____
2. 98 – 57 = ____
3. 87 – 39 = ____
4. 70 – 28 = ____
5. 275 – 56 = ____

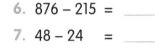

6. 876 – 215 = ____
7. 48 – 24 = ____
8. 163 – 35 = ____
9. 790 – 343 = ____
10. 194 – 49 = ____

/10

C Mental Maths — In your head.

1. $\frac{1}{2}$ litre = ____ ml
2. $2\frac{1}{4} < \frac{14}{4}$. True ☐ False ☐
3. 25, 50, 75, ____
4. Draw the net of a cylinder. ____
5. What are the chances of picking an odd number between 1 and 11? ____ in ____
6.  6cm Area = 24 cm². Length = 6 cm. Width = ____ cm
7. 9 x 9 = ____
8. 10% of a century = ____
9. A new shirt costs €20. There is a 20% reduction in a sale. What is the new price? ____

10. Michelle has 84 coins. Antoinette has 46. How many do they have altogether? ____
11. Treble 41. ____
12. ⌣ This shape is a ____.
13. Circle the symmetrical letter. r A f
14. 8, 6, 4, ____, 0, ⁻2, ____, ⁻6
15. How many faces on a cuboid? ____
16. How many seconds in three and a half minutes? ____
17. How many degrees in 3 right angles? ____
18. 179° = an ____ angle
19. How many 50c coins make up €6? ____
20. 4 ⟌ 9·604 = ____

/20

D Vocabulary

Wordsearch.

1. The value of 8 in 4,821 is eight _ _ _ _ _ _ _.

2. The _ _ _ _ _ _ _ of 3 and 7 is 21.

3. 90° = a _ _ _ _ _ _ angle

4. 6 is the _ _ _ _ _ _ _ of 4, 6 and 8.

5. The third month of the year is _ _ _ _ _ _.

6. $\frac{12}{16}$ = _ _ _ _ _ quarters

7. 19 is a _ _ _ _ _ _ number.

8. 98 is a _ _ _ _ _ _ _ _ of 7.

9. _ _ _ _ x eight = thirty-two.

f	t	p	r	o	d	u	c	t	p
o	h	c	r	a	m	e	m	l	d
u	m	y	r	t	g	g	f	r	e
r	t	s	y	a	v	k	r	h	r
y	r	l	r	x	h	q	x	x	d
u	k	e	r	i	g	h	t	c	n
i	v	n	c	s	v	s	m	w	u
a	m	u	l	t	i	p	l	e	h
p	r	i	m	e	e	e	r	h	t
i	r	w	i	d	t	h	h	a	t

E Mental Maths

In your head.

1. Write 3·6 litres in millilitres. _____ mL

2. What is the perimeter of a square with side 12 cm? _____

3. Write 20 minutes before 06:15. _____

4. 0·75, 0·7, _____, 0·6, 0·55

5. Round 6·08 to the nearest tenth. _____

6. $5\frac{1}{4} > \frac{18}{4}$. True ☐ False ☐

7. Write the Roman numeral for 25. _____

8. $\frac{1}{3}$ of 2 dozen. _____

9. ⁻9, ⁻6, ⁻3, _____, ⁺3, _____, ⁺9

10. Write 0·3 as a fraction. _____

11. Write $\frac{7}{10}$ as a decimal. _____

12. Is 336 divisible evenly by 8? _____

13. 24 children were surveyed as to their favourite snack bars. The results were shown on a pie chart.

Pow Wow / Apple Snap / Nutty Bunch / Orange Dream / Jupiter

(a) How many liked Apple Snap? _____

(b) What was the favourite bar? _____

(c) What were the three least favourite bars? _____ _____ _____

(d) How many more children preferred Pow Wow to Jupiter? _____

14. Halve 72. _____

15. 898,989 + 9 = _____

/15

F Puzzle

Problem of the week.

Julie plants 7 rose bushes so that they form 3 straight lines with 3 bushes in each line. Draw the formation of the 7 bushes.

G Topic — Weight. In your head.

1. $\frac{1}{2}$ kg = _____ g
2. $1\frac{3}{4}$ kg = _____ g
3. $\frac{1}{10}$ kg = _____ g
4. $3\frac{1}{4}$ kg = _____ g
5. 2·8 kg = _____ g
6. 1,456 g = _____ kg
7. 542 g = _____ kg
8. $4\frac{23}{1000}$ kg = _____ g
9. 2,065 g = _____ kg _____ g
10. $\frac{3}{10}$ kg + $\frac{1}{4}$ kg = _____ g

11. 10 g = _____ kg
12. What is the difference between $3\frac{1}{2}$ kg and 2,300 g? _____ g
13. 2 kg – 1 kg 250 g = _____ g
14. 4,000 g = _____ kg
15. 2 kg 34 g = _____ g
16. $\frac{12}{1000}$ kg = _____ g
17. 0·002 kg = _____ g
18. 9 g = _____ kg
19. $2\frac{1}{2}$ kg = _____ g
20. 3·7 kg = _____ g

/20

H Topic — Weight. Problem solving. In your copy.

1. Cornflakes weigh 750 g. Salt weights 865 g. What is the difference in their weights? _____
2. A sheep weighs 63 kg 721 g. A man weighs 96 kg 200 g. Which is heavier, 3 sheep or 2 men? _____
3. (a) What is the total weight of 8 bags each weighing 3·965 kg? _____
   (b) How much less than 35·500 kg is the weight of the 8 bags? _____
4. A box full of school dictionaries weighs 13 kg 450 g. Weights of 2·014 kg, 3,614 g and 2 kg 34 g are taken out. What is the weight of the box now? _____
5. $\frac{1}{4}$ of Mary's weight is 9 kg 260 g. Ciaran is $\frac{3}{4}$ of Mary's weight.
   (a) How much does Ciaran weigh? _____
   (b) How much do the two weigh altogether? _____

6. 9 boxes of tomatoes weighs a total of 34 kg 650 g.
   (a) What is the weight of just one box? _____
   (b) What is the weight of 4 boxes? _____
7. What change would you get out of €10 if you bought 500 g of tomatoes at €3·20 a kg and 500 g mushrooms at €4·80 a kg? _____

/7

I. Mental Maths

Beat the clock.

1. Simplify $\frac{8}{10}$. _____

2. What change will I get from €5 if I spend €3·63? _____

3. 37, 41, 45, _____, _____

4. Simplify $\frac{25}{100}$. _____

5. Write $8\frac{23}{100}$ as a decimal. _____

6. Put in the correct sign.
   6 x 8 _____ 7 x 7

7. $\frac{7}{10} + \frac{8}{100} =$ _____ %

8. Write $3\frac{5}{10}$ as a decimal. _____

9. 66, 71, 76, _____, _____

10. What change will I get from €5 if I spend €2·08? _____

11. $\frac{0}{10} + \frac{1}{100} =$ _____ %

12. 16 + 18 _____ 17 x 2

13. 131 minutes = _____ hours _____ minutes

14. Simplify $\frac{3}{6}$. _____

15. What change will I get from €5 if I spend €1·79? _____

16. 2 hours 15 minutes = _____ minutes.

17. Write $56\frac{4}{5}$ as a decimal. _____

18. 27 + 29 _____ 29 + 27

19. $\frac{2}{10} + \frac{9}{100} =$ _____ %

20. 18, 25, 32, _____, _____

 /20

J. Code Cracker

Each problem has a letter. Solve the problem and put the letter into the grid to reveal the message! You may use your calculator.

M $= \frac{2}{3}$ of 999 = _____

K $= (52 \times 63) \div 12 =$ _____

T $= (2,148 \div 6) \times 2 =$ _____

Y $= (999 \div 9) + 90 =$ _____

I $= 21 \times 21 =$ _____

U $= (54 \times 13) - 200 =$ _____

A $= (7,689 - 6,999) + 20 =$ _____

E $= (2,585 \div 5) =$ _____

H $= (7,290 \div 9) =$ _____

W $= 30 \times 15 \times 2 =$ _____

S $= \frac{2}{7}$ of 2,149 = _____

N $= 4,955 \div 5 =$ _____

L $= (64 \div 8) \times (12 \div 2) =$ _____

666	710	273	517

810	710	201

900	810	441	48	517

716	810	517

614	502	991

614	810	441	991	517	614

K. Puzzle

Haretown and Tortoiseville are 44 km apart. A hare runs at 8 km per hour from Haretown to Tortoiseville. A tortoise walks at 3 km per hour from Tortoiseville to Haretown. If they both start at the same time how many kilometres will the hare travel before meeting the tortoise? _____

A Table Time — Beat the clock.

1. (14 x 3) x 2 = ____
2. (6 + 19) + 24 = ____
3. (29 – 14) ÷ 3 = ____
4. (81 ÷ 9) x 3 = ____
5. (6 x 5) – 2 = ____
6. (29 + 41) ÷ 5 = ____
7. (15 – 5) + 36 = ____
8. (16 ÷ 4) + 23 = ____
9. (8 x 5) x 2 = ____
10. (31 – 17) – 6 = ____
11. (16 + 16) ÷ 4 = ____
12. (21 ÷ 3) x 6 = ____
13. (2 x 17) – 8 = ____
14. (51 – 16) ÷ 5 = ____
15. (30 ÷ 6) x 9 = ____
16. (41 + 15) – 10 = ____
17. (6 x 9) + 25 = ____
18. (72 ÷ 8) + 16 = ____
19. (37 – 18) – 2 = ____
20. (47 + 15) ÷ 0 = ____

/20

B Try this — Use your calculator.

Increase

Increase 250 by 20%
Key in 250 + 20%
Answer: 300

Increase:
1. 150 by 30% = ____
2. 750 by 5% = ____
3. 100 by 10% = ____
4. 180 by 36% = ____
5. 495 by 15% = ____
6. 370 by 29% = ____
7. 285 by 20% = ____
8. 220 by 19% = ____
9. 496 by 25% = ____
10. 850 by 40% = ____

/10

C Mental Maths — In your head.

1. 1 apple weighs 35g. How much would 10 apples weigh? ____ g
2. €100 – €55·50 = € ____
3. 500 ÷ 10 = ____
4. Double 680. ____
5. $\frac{51}{100}$ = ____ %
6. 5·00 x 0·05 = ____
7. 1 + 0·2 + 4·04 = ____
8. Name this shape. ____
9. 8cm 7cm Area = ____ cm².
10. Which scales would you use to weigh a cat? Kitchen ☐ bathroom ☐
11. Find the sum of 10·111, 10·321 and 10·481. ____
12. 11 x 0 = ____
13. 25% of 400 = ____
14. How many faces on a hemisphere? ____
15. 450, 900, 1,350, ____
16. What is the probability of picking an even red number from a deck of cards? ____ in ____
17. What is this shape? ____
18. 7, 5, 3, 1, ⁻1, ____, ____
19. Kay swam 50 metres 8 times. How far did she swim altogether? ____
20. There is a 25% sale in Jenny's Boutique. The sale price of a skirt is €24. What was the original price? ____

/20

D Vocabulary

Wordsearch.

1. [diagram] This is the net of a

   _ _ _ _ _ _ _ _.

2. 14 days = a

   _ _ _ _ _ _ _ _ _

3. A full turn = a full

   _ _ _ _ _ _ _ _

4. The eleventh month of the year is

   _ _ _ _ _ _ _ _.

5. The perimeter of a

   _ _ _ _ _ _ is called its circumference.

6. 10 years = a

   _ _ _ _ _ _

7. 100 years = a

   _ _ _ _ _ _ _

8. 7 is an odd number. 4 is an _ _ _ _ number.

9. Diameter = twice the

   _ _ _ _ _ _

```
z  r  e  b  m  e  v  o  n  b
v  k  e  m  d  e  p  i  t  s
k  l  d  c  z  l  i  n  h  u
g  d  a  s  m  c  i  d  g  i
r  t  c  n  g  r  b  y  i  d
o  g  e  g  i  i  s  j  n  a
y  v  d  o  u  c  p  s  t  r
e  c  y  l  i  n  d  e  r  d
r  o  t  a  t  i  o  n  o  n
e  y  r  u  t  n  e  c  f  z
```

E Mental Maths

In your head.

1. $3\frac{3}{4}$ kg = _____ g = 3· _____ kg

2. $2 \times$ _____ = 24

3. $^+20$, $^+15$, $^+10$, $^+5$, 0, _____, _____, $^-15$

4. $313{,}333 - 4 =$ _____

5. Toss a coin. What are the chances of it landing on a head? _____ in _____

6. Write the number one million one hundred and eleven thousand one hundred and eleven. _____

7. A Turn this letter 270° anticlockwise. _____

8. How many hours in $3\frac{1}{2}$ days? _____

9. 19 m = _____ km

10. 100 g cheese cost 90c. How much for 1 kg? _____

11. How much for 3 kg of the cheese in question 10? _____

12. $3 + 5{\cdot}05 + 0{\cdot}1 =$ _____

13. What is the 4th angle of this quadrilateral: 50°, 120°, 70°, _____°

14. $\frac{2}{3}$ of 81 = _____

15. What is opposite of south on the compass?

   _____

_____ /15

F Puzzle

Problem of the week.

In the farm animal section of the zoo $\frac{1}{3}$ of the animals, the gerbils, are mixed with $\frac{1}{6}$ of the animals, the hamsters. Next door $\frac{1}{3}$ of the animals, the rabbits, are kept. The remainder of the animals, the guinea pigs, are in a pen of their own. There are 6 guinea pigs. How many of each animal are there? How many animals altogether?

G Topic — Percentages. In your head.

1. 0·03 = ____%
2. $\frac{3}{4}$ = ____%
3. 0·97 = ____%
4. $\frac{1}{3}$ = ____%
5. 20% of 450 = ____
6. I spent $37\frac{1}{2}$% of €48. How much have I left? ____
7. Add $12\frac{1}{2}$% of 800 and $33\frac{1}{3}$% of 363. ____
8. Reduce €150 by 20%. ____
9. Increase 55 by 20%. ____
10. What is the price of a jacket worth €48 less $12\frac{1}{2}$% discount? ____
11. In a 25% sale a dress sold for €30. What was the original price? ____
12. $\frac{2}{3}$ of my money is €90. What is the whole amount? ____
13. $\frac{1}{8}$ of John's stamp collection is 25. How many stamps has he altogether? ____
14. Add $\frac{1}{4}$ of 72 and $\frac{1}{5}$ of 90. ____
15. Increase 180 by 50%. ____

/15

H Topic — Percentages. Problem solving. In your copy.

1. George bought a television for €384. The dealer offered a 25% discount if he paid in cash.
   (a) What was the reduction? ____
   (b) How much would George have to pay? ____

2. Find the sale price for each of these items.

Item	Original Price	Reduction	Selling Price
Stereo	€360	10%	
Washing machine	€435	20%	
Dining room table & chairs	€693	$33\frac{1}{3}$%	
Games console	€155	20%	

3. Kate bought a coat reduced from €255 by 20% and a pair of boots for €130 reduced by $12\frac{1}{2}$%. How much did she save altogether? ____

4. A newsagent sold 1,464 newspapers on Monday. He sold $12\frac{1}{2}$% less on Tuesday.
   (a) How many did he sell on Tuesday? ____
   (b) How many papers did he sell altogether on Monday and Tuesday? ____

5. Sean was buying a new car for €34,380. If he chose the diesel engine it would be 10% dearer. How much would the diesel car cost? ____

6. Mum gave John, aged 12, €5, Mary, aged 10, €3·50 and Kevin, aged 8, €3 pocket money each week. She agreed to increase the amount for each by 20%.
   (a) How much extra did each get? ____
   (b) How much extra did Mum have to pay altogether? ____

/6

 Mental Maths

Beat the clock.

Write these a.m./p.m. times as 24-hour time.

1. 3:55 p.m. _____
2. 11:15 a.m. _____
3. 1:45 p.m. _____
4. 3:56 a.m. _____
5. 12:10 p.m. _____
6. 12:30 a.m. _____
7. 10:40 p.m. _____
8. 8:06 a.m. _____
9. 4:35 a.m. _____
10. 11:22 p.m. _____

Write these 24-hour times in a.m./p.m. time.

1. 09:25 _____
2. 11:36 _____
3. 00:01 _____
4. 12:55 _____
5. 17:36 _____
6. 19:51 _____
7. 23:10 _____
8. 19:45 _____
9. 22:56 _____
10. 03:38 _____

/20

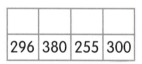 Code Cracker

Each problem has a letter. Solve the problem and put the letter into the grid to reveal the message! You may use your calculator.

M = $(148 \div 2) \times 4$ = _____

N = 15×17 = _____

H = $\frac{3}{5}$ of 285 = _____

S = $21{\cdot}5 \times 12$ = _____

E = $3{,}896 - 3{,}792$ = _____

I = 75×5 = _____

T = $\frac{6}{8}$ of 800 = _____

O = $\frac{2}{5}$ of 575 = _____

A = 19×20 = _____

Y = 12×25 = _____

D = $1{,}265 - 1{,}200$ = _____

K = 58×5 = _____

L = 12×17 = _____

G = $(350 \times 10) \div 5$ = _____

W = $57 \times (8 \div 2)$ = _____

R = 25×25 = _____

296	380	255	300

171	380	255	65	258

296	380	290	104

204	375	700	171	600

228	230	625	290

Puzzle

The sweet factory is making gobstoppers. To make them more interesting every second gobstopper gets a red layer outside, every third gobstopper gets a blue star printed on its outside layer and every fifth gobstopper gets a green stripe added. Out of the first 100 gobstoppers how many will have all three decorations, the red outside with a star and green stripe?

Hint: Use a hundred square and cross off the multiples.

A Table Time

Beat the clock.

1. (6 x 7) + 3 = ____
2. (24 ÷ 8) – 1 = ____
3. (81 + 16) – 38 = ____
4. (91 – 17) ÷ 2 = ____
5. (8 x 6) ÷ 2 = ____
6. (16 + 16) x 3 = ____
7. (63 – 14) – 15 = ____

8. (17 + 18) + 24 = ____
9. (13 x 3) x 2 = ____
10. (32 ÷ 4) – 16 = ____
11. (6 ÷ 6) ÷ 1 = ____
12. (17 + 34) + 12 = ____
13. (19 x 4) x 2 = ____
14. (39 – 16) – 15 = ____

15. (13 + 21) + 16 = ____
16. (48 ÷ 4) x 2 = ____
17. (19 + 26) ÷ 5 = ____
18. (16 x 10) ÷ 8 = ____
19. (24 – 7) x 4 = ____
20. (100 ÷ 10) + 25 = ____

/20

B Try this

Use your calculator.

 Decrease

Decrease 80 by 10%

Key in 80 – 10%

Answer: 72

Decrease:

1. 395 by 60% ____
2. 250 by 40% ____
3. 280 by 10% ____
4. 160 by 15% ____
5. 800 by 50% ____

6. 436 by 75% ____
7. 200 by 10% ____
8. 165 by 80% ____
9. 490 by 30% ____
10. 285 by 20% ____

/10

C Mental Maths

In your head.

1. $\frac{7}{12} - \frac{1}{4}$ = ____
2. Mark ⁻2° on the thermometer.
3. In Brid's Toyshop there is a 20% discount. The sale price for a doll is €48. What was the full price? ____
4. Halve 230. ____
5. Add 13·61 and 78·409. ____
6. $12\frac{1}{2}$% of 48 = ____
7. 11 x 11 = ____
8. Write 10 as a Roman numeral. ____
9. 0·5 x 5 = ____
10. 70 x 80 = ____

11. (4 x 50c) + (6 x 10c) + (8 x 20c) = € ____
12. 49 = a x a. a = ____
13. (F) Turn this letter 180° anticlockwise. ____
14. A nonagon has ____ sides.
15. Write 17:20 in the 12 hour clock. ____
16. Write the number 1 before 1,800. ____
17. $\frac{1}{5}$, $\frac{1}{10}$, $\frac{1}{20}$, $\frac{1}{40}$, ____
18. John has 86 marbles. Ben has 112. How many do they have altogether? ____
19. 22 x 0 = ____
20. (9 x 7) + (4 x 5) = ____

/20

D Vocabulary — Wordsearch.

1. Cent is to euro as centimetre is to _ _ _ _ _.

2. How many degrees in $\frac{1}{3}$ of a right angle? _ _ _ _ _ _

3. 16·5 is _ _ _ _ _ _ _ than 16·05.

4. 300 seconds = _ _ _ _ minutes

5. The perimeter of a square is 16 cm. One side is _ _ _ _ cm long.

6. 10 years = a _ _ _ _ _ _

7. _ _ _ _ _ _ _ _ means straight up.

8. 1000 millilitres = 1 _ _ _ _ _

z	b	s	d	e	c	a	d	e	c
h	h	p	r	a	l	c	c	v	f
a	h	a	l	k	e	t	v	c	j
m	p	r	e	r	y	o	w	m	o
b	m	v	t	t	b	h	t	m	w
p	i	i	r	m	e	t	r	e	x
f	l	i	r	e	t	a	e	r	g
t	h	u	g	o	s	v	n	q	g
t	v	e	r	t	i	c	a	l	k
z	c	g	s	w	p	r	u	o	f

E Mental Maths — In your head.

1. $\frac{6}{9} - \frac{2}{6} =$ _____

2. Round 9·99 to the nearest tenth. _____

3. 18 + 1·8 + 0·18 = _____

4. $\frac{4}{6} + \frac{5}{6} + \frac{4}{6} = \frac{}{6} =$ _____ (mixed number)

5. 8·00 x 0·8 = _____

6. Simplify $\frac{15}{30}$. _____

7. Can a circle tessellate? _____

8. 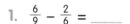 This is a _____ triangle.

9. €70 – €25·40 = _____

10. Treble 50. _____

11. Is 436 divisible by 9 with no remainder? _____

12. Write the prime numbers between 40 and 50. _____ _____ _____

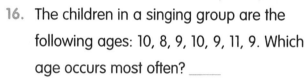

13. $\frac{8}{9} = \frac{}{27}$

14. 27, 21, 15, _____, _____

15. 70 + 40 + 80 = _____

16. The children in a singing group are the following ages: 10, 8, 9, 10, 9, 11, 9. Which age occurs most often? _____

17. What is the value of the 3 in 6·03? _____

18. Majella had 72 sweets. Christine ate 24 of them. How many were left? _____

19. Find the average of 4, 2, 8, 5 and 6. _____

20. What is the area of a square with side 10 cm. _____ cm²

/20

F Puzzle — Problem of the week.

For doing jobs, Dad agrees to give Joe 1c the first day, 2c the second day, then 4c, then 8c and so on. How much would Joe have after 15 days? _____

G Topic — Graphs. In your head.

1. How many degrees in a full turn? ____

2. What fraction of 360° is 120°? ____

3. $\frac{1}{4}$ of 360° = ____

4. What fraction of 360° is 60°? ____

5. Look at the graph and answer the questions.

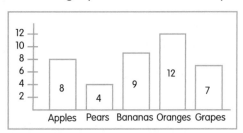

(a) How many pupils took part in the survey?

____

(b) Which was the most popular fruit? ____

(c) How many preferred oranges to grapes?

____

(d) Which fruit was $\frac{1}{3}$ as popular as oranges?

____

(e) Which fruit was preferred by twice as many pupils as pears? ____

6. Look at the pie chart and answer the questions. There are 36 children in the class.

(a) How many prefer football? ____

(b) How many prefer hurling? ____

(c) How many prefer rugby? ____

(d) How many more prefer football than rugby? ____

(e) How many children prefer hurling to tennis? ____

7. How many degrees in half a rotation? ____

8. $\frac{1}{6}$ of a rotation = ____°

9. $\frac{1}{8}$ of a rotation = ____°

10. 5 out of 20 children prefer cats. What fraction of a pie chart is this? ____

/10

H Topic — Graphs. Problem solving. In your copy.

1. Bar chart.

(a) List the sports in order of popularity. ____

(b) Which was the most popular? ____

(c) Which was the least popular? ____

(d) Two sports were twice as popular as another – name one of them. ____

(e) How many children are in the group altogether? ____

2. Line graph.

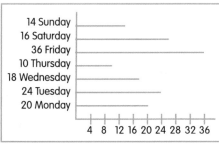

(a) How many more litres of milk were sold on Friday than Tuesday? ____

(b) How many litres were sold over the week? ____

(c) What was the average number of litres sold per day? (Round your answer to the nearest whole number.) ____

(d) Which days sold more than the average? ____

/9

I Mental Maths

Beat the clock.

1. $\frac{1}{2} = \frac{}{8}$

2. $\frac{3}{4} = \frac{}{8}$

3. $\frac{3}{9} = \frac{1}{}$

4. $\frac{1}{2} + \frac{1}{4} =$ _____

5. $\frac{1}{3} + \frac{1}{6} =$ _____

6. $\frac{3}{8} - \frac{1}{4} =$ _____

7. $\frac{4}{8} = \frac{}{2}$

8. Write $\frac{5}{2}$ as a mixed number. _____

9. $3\frac{1}{2} = \frac{}{2}$

10. $3\frac{4}{5} = \frac{}{5}$

11. $\frac{1}{4} = \frac{}{12}$

12. $\frac{2}{3} = \frac{}{12}$

13. $\frac{9}{12} = \frac{3}{}$

14. $\frac{1}{4} + \frac{3}{4} =$ _____

15. $\frac{5}{6} - \frac{1}{3} =$ _____

16. $\frac{3}{4} - \frac{1}{2} =$ _____

17. $\frac{8}{12} = \frac{}{3}$

18. Write $\frac{7}{3}$ as a mixed number. _____

19. $5\frac{1}{3} = \frac{}{3}$

20. Write $\frac{17}{5}$ as a mixed number. _____

/20

J Code Cracker

Each problem has a letter. Solve the problem and put the letter into the grid to reveal the message!
You may use your calculator.

F $= \frac{2}{3}$ of 126 = _____

R $= 3{,}456 - 2{,}978 =$ _____

Y $= 38 \times 9 =$ _____

I $= \frac{1}{2}$ of 354 = _____

S $= 145 \times 5 =$ _____

G $= (148 \times 7) \div 2 =$ _____

A $= (45 \times 2) \div 3 =$ _____

W $= (1{,}798 \times 3) \div 6 =$ _____

H $= \frac{4}{5}$ of 745 = _____

L $= 147 \times 5 =$ _____

E $= (37 \times 8) \div 4 =$ _____

N $= 9{,}874 - 9{,}452 =$ _____

84	30	478

30	899	30	342

596	177	735	735	725

30	478	74

518	478	74	74	422	74	478

K Puzzle

It takes 5 monkeys 5 minutes to eat 5 bananas.
How many minutes would it take 2 monkeys to
eat 2 bananas?

A. Table Time — Beat the clock.

1. $(28 \div 7) \div 2$ = _____
2. $(24 \times 2) + 37$ = _____
3. $(17 + 18) \times 5$ = _____
4. $(75 - 25) - 14$ = _____
5. $(81 \div 9) + 15$ = _____
6. $(35 \times 2) \div 7$ = _____
7. $(15 + 28) - 16$ = _____

8. $(63 - 7) \times 5$ = _____
9. $(100 \div 10) \div 2$ = _____
10. $(42 \times 3) + 15$ = _____
11. $(8 + 8) \times 5$ = _____
12. $(100 - 73) - 9$ = _____
13. $(22 \div 2) + 18$ = _____
14. $(14 \times 5) \div 10$ = _____

15. $(16 + 35) \times 15$ = _____
16. $(98 - 63) \times 2$ = _____
17. $(63 \div 7) \div 3$ = _____
18. $(18 \times 5) - 48$ = _____
19. $(19 + 21) \times 3$ = _____
20. $(58 - 16) + 34$ = _____

/20

B. Try this — Multiplying by 11 up to 19.

x by 11 to 19

24 x 15

$(24 \times 10) + (24 \times 5)$

240 + 120 = 362

1. 63×14 = _____
2. 72×19 = _____
3. 51×12 = _____
4. 83×19 = _____
5. 99×16 = _____

6. 45×17 = _____
7. 34×15 = _____
8. 48×13 = _____
9. 26×14 = _____
10. 17×18 = _____

/10

C. Mental Maths — In your head.

1. $8 + 11 = 6 + f$. f = _____
2. Write 10:25 a.m. in 24 hour time. _____
3. If you walked for an hour and covered 6 km, how far did you go in 10 minutes? _____
4. Is 8·45 nearer to 8 or 9? _____
5. $1 \cdot 5 \times 6$ = _____
6. Write the Roman numeral for 12. _____
7. A bike costs €225. There is a 20% sale. What will the bike cost now? _____
8. $5 + 0 \cdot 3 + 0 \cdot 8$ = _____
9. Find the average of 20, 10, 30, 15 and 5. _____
10. Farmer Joe has 12 sheep. Each sheep has 2 lambs. How many lambs has he? _____

11. What direction is opposite south-east? _____
12. The radius of a circle is 17 cm. Find the diameter. _____ cm
13. $3 \frac{1}{2} = \frac{8}{2}$. True ☐ False ☐
14. A cylinder has _____ edges.
15. How many lines of symmetry in a regular hexagon? _____
16. Round 212·17 to the nearest tenth. _____
17. Treble 94. _____
18. 25×100 = _____
19. Round 6,882 to the nearest hundred. _____
20. How many 10c coins do you need to make €5? _____

/20

D Vocabulary

Wordsearch.

1. Second is to minute as _ _ _ _ _ _ is to hour.

2. An oblique line is _ _ _ _ _ _ _ _ _.

3. 07:04 is four minutes past seven _ _.

4. Sixteen divided by four is _ _ _ _.

5. The seventh month of the year is _ _ _ _.

7. Treble twenty is _ _ _ _ _.

8. 7:45 = a _ _ _ _ _ _ _ _ to eight

9. A, B, C, D and E are all symmetrical _ _ _ _ _ _ _.

10. This is the net of what shape?

_ _ _ _

o	i	n	s	i	x	t	y	c	f
y	e	t	u	n	i	m	d	d	o
e	n	i	n	b	z	j	z	l	u
j	l	a	n	o	g	a	i	d	r
m	u	u	o	o	m	t	w	f	e
c	g	l	r	e	t	r	a	u	q
f	u	c	y	m	e	q	x	b	f
t	t	b	f	x	k	a	m	x	l
b	q	s	e	b	m	x	m	u	g
m	l	e	t	t	e	r	s	t	q

E Mental Maths

In your head.

1. (15 x 10c) + (14 x 50c) = € _____

2. $\frac{6}{10} = \frac{}{50}$

3. Round 2,769 to the nearest hundred. _____

4. Write the number three million three hundred and three thousand and three. _____

5. How many degrees in each angle of an equilateral triangle? _____

6. How many angles in a hexagon? _____

7. What are the chances of picking a black picture card from a deck of cards? _____ in _____

8. $\frac{}{24} = \frac{2}{3}$

9. Write the next 2 composite numbers after 14. _____ _____

10. Write the number thirty six point one eight. _____

11. $\frac{3}{5} + \frac{2}{5} + \frac{4}{5} =$ _____ (mixed number)

12. 80 x 0·05 = _____

13. 4 halves of a cake makes _____ whole cakes.

14. If Niamh cycled 12 km in an hour, how far would she cycle in $\frac{1}{4}$ of an hour? _____

15. Round 4,971 to the nearest ten. _____

/15

F Puzzle

Problem of the week.

What does each letter stand for?

```
   77
 x  B
 ----
  38B
```

B = ☐

```
   3G
 x  6
 ----
  22G
```

G = ☐

Topic — Symmetry. In your head.

1. Is the letter A symmetrical? ____
2. Draw in the axis of symmetry.
3. Complete the reflection of this shape.
4. How many axes of symmetry has a square? 2 ☐ 3 ☐ 4 ☐
5. Circle the numbers that are symmetrical.
   1 2 3 5 7 8
6. Circle the letters that are symmetrical.
   C D F G H S
7. Draw in the axis of symmetry.
8. Draw the other half of this picture.

9. Is an equilateral triangle symmetrical? ____
10. Is the number 1,001 symmetrical? ____
11. Draw in an axis of symmetry.
12. Is a parallelogram symmetrical? ____
13. Circle the symmetrical letters.
    X Z P O F
14. How many axes of symmetry does a rectangle have? ____
15. Draw in the axes of symmetry.

/15

 Topic — Symmetry. Problem solving. In your copy.

1. Draw in the lines of symmetry.

2. Complete the reflections of each of these.

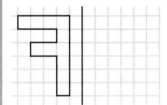 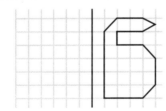

3. Which of the following are symmetrical?

F A P B E H
8 D S M 3 Z

Draw in their axes of symmetry.

4. Did you notice anything about the number of axes of symmetry and the number of sides of equal length in the shapes in question 1? What is it? ____
5. Did you notice anything about the number of axes of symmetry for the circle? ____
6. Could you give another name for the axis of symmetry in a circle? It begins with d. ____
7. What does infinity mean? Why do we use this word when counting the axes of symmetry of a circle? ____

/7

Mental Maths

Beat the clock.

Write in short form (e.g. 3rd April 2008 = 3/4/08)

1. 16th June 2009. ____
2. 26th July 2019. ____
3. 14th September 2010. ____
4. 17th March 2009. ____
5. 31st May 2020. ____
6. 6th August 2041. ____

7. 14th February 2014. ____
8. 26th September 2000. ____
9. 7th April 2004. ____
10. 17th January 2008. ____

Write in words (e.g. 3/4/08 = 3rd April 2008)

11. 6/12/06. ____
12. 16/5/10. ____

13. 8/1/09. ____
14. 22/11/14. ____
15. 28/6/20. ____
16. 4/11/10. ____
17. 30/4/06. ____
18. 13/3/15. ____
19. 25/12/08. ____
20. 9/4/10. ____

/20

J Code Cracker

Each problem has a letter. Solve the problem and put the letter into the grid to reveal the message! You may use your calculator.

O = (2,177 ÷ 7) x 3 = ____
E = (1,505 ÷ 5) x 2 = ____
A = (264 ÷ 2) x 5 = ____
T = 10 x (80 ÷ 8) = ____

H = 25 x 15 x 2 = ____
L = (6 ÷ 2) x 180 = ____
N = (1,050 ÷ 25) x 18 = ____
M = (6,248 – 4,976) ÷ 2 = ____

S = (497 ÷ 7) x 11 = ____
I = (568 ÷ 8) x 10 = ____
R = 17,280 ÷ (40 x 2) = ____
G = 23 x 24 = ____

660

216	933	540	540	710	756	552

781	100	933	756	602

552	660	100	750	602	216	781

756	933

636	933	781	781

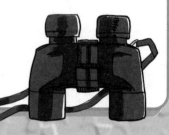

K Puzzle

A teacher has 25 sticks of chalk. She uses 1 a day but when it reaches $\frac{1}{5}$ its normal size it is too small to hold. However, she puts all the small pieces together to make a full stick. How many days will 25 sticks last? ____

A Table Time

Beat the clock.

1. (64 x 3) ÷ 6   = ____
2. (79 – 24) + 75 = ____
3. (28 ÷ 4) – 3   = ____
4. (16 + 29) x 5 = ____
5. (30 x 3) ÷ 9   = ____
6. (15 + 45) – 29 = ____
7. (25 – 14) x 6 = ____

8. (96 ÷ 8) + 18 = ____
9. (49 – 33) ÷ 4 = ____
10. (16 x 8) – 39 = ____
11. (99 ÷ 11) – 2 = ____
12. (63 ÷ 9) + 38 = ____
13. (46 x 2) x 3   = ____
14. (57 – 8) ÷ 7   = ____

15. (12 x 5) + 31   = ____
16. (47 – 25) – 10 = ____
17. (86 – 48) x 3   = ____
18. (24 x 5) + 100 = ____
19. (300 ÷ 5) ÷ 4 = ____
20. (27 x 6) – 34   = ____

/20

B Try this

Estimate means a good guess!

Estimate

Round the numbers to the nearest 10 and calculate.

68 + 57 → 70 + 60 = 130

89 x 17 → 90 x 20 = 1800

1. 37 + 25 → ____
2. 4,216 + 834 → ____
3. 7 x 8 x 13 → ____
4. 396 ÷ 41 → ____
5. 74 – 29 → ____

6. 16 x 8 → ____
7. 147 – 83 → ____
8. 215 ÷ 8 → ____
9. 240 – 138 → ____
10. 20 x 8 → ____

/10

C Mental Maths

In your head.

1. This is the net of which 3D shape? ____
2. Draw 2 lines perpendicular to each other.
3. Write the next prime number after 13. ____
4. 0·6 x 0·4 = ____
5. Ann earns €110 per day. How much does she earn in ten days? ____
6. Find $\frac{1}{7}$ of a fortnight. ____
7. $3\frac{1}{2}$ litres = ____ mL
8. 6, 17, 28, 39, 50, ____
9.  Find the perimeter of this shape. ____ cm

10. 50° a   a = ____ °
11. A heptagon has ____ sides.
12. Write in order from largest to smallest.
    $\frac{11}{12}$ $\frac{7}{8}$ $\frac{1}{2}$ $\frac{5}{6}$ $\frac{3}{4}$ ____
13. 18 is a multiple of 3. True ☐ False ☐
14. 6·4 ÷ 4 = ____
15. The angles in all triangles add up ____ °.
16. If Noirín walks 1·5 km in 20 minutes, how far will she walk in an hour? ____
17. 80 x 0·03 = ____
18. Mark the temperature ⁻1. ____
19. $\frac{3}{5} + \frac{4}{5} + \frac{4}{5} =$ ____ (mixed number)
20. y + 11 = 50. y = ____

/20

D Vocabulary

Wordsearch.

1. 15 minutes = a _ _ _ _ _ _ _ of an hour

2. In mathematical language, a clown's hat is a _ _ _ _ _.

3. 1,000 ml = one _ _ _ _ _

4. _ _ _ _ _ _ x twelve = one hundred and forty-four

5. _ _ _ _ _ 5c coins make up €1.

6. A _ _ _ _ _ _ _ _ _ is a 5 sided shape.

7. There are 366 days in a _ _ _ _ year.

8. The eighth month of the year is _ _ _ _ _ _ .

9. _ _ _ _ _ _ _ _ _ means straight up.

t	f	d	w	m	z	k	b	m	k
z	e	n	p	a	e	l	p	r	z
c	o	n	e	v	d	n	w	e	o
i	h	c	q	e	s	o	r	t	v
u	v	o	r	r	y	g	t	r	t
e	e	t	b	t	z	a	s	a	w
w	i	k	n	i	d	t	u	u	e
l	u	e	a	c	s	n	g	q	l
n	w	n	u	a	z	e	u	g	v
t	s	x	h	l	z	p	a	g	e

E Mental Maths

In your head.

1. This is a net of a _____.

2. A reflex angle is bigger than _____°.

3. Draw an oblique line. _____

4. How many edges on a sphere? _____

5. Write the last prime number before 100. _____

6. $(36 ÷ 9) + (45 ÷ 5) =$ _____

7. $9 = b \times b.$ $b =$ _____

8. $16 ÷ 4 =$ _____

9. Write $\frac{25}{8}$ as a mixed number. _____

10. $0·8 = 85\%$. True ☐ False ☐

11. Circle the multiples of 3.   21   24   28   30

12. 3,000, 300, 30, 3, _____

13. Write the number three thousand one hundred and one point three. _____

14. $\frac{160}{100} = 1·6 =$ _____ %

15. Write in order from smallest to largest. 0·25 0·4 0·20 _____ _____ _____

16. Round 6,898 to the nearest thousand. _____

17. Patrick earns €15 per hour. How much does he earn in 5 hours? _____

18. A square pyramid has _____ faces.

19. Write in ascending order. 0·3 0·32 0·03 0·23 _____ _____ _____ _____

20. Write the factors of 22. _____ _____ _____ _____

/20

F Puzzle

Problem of the week.

A bee wants to collect pollen from all nine flowers without stopping. How can he do this by flying in only four straight lines? _____

Topic — Capacity. In your head.

1. 2,000 ml = _____ l

2. 500 ml = 0·_____ l = $\frac{1}{}$ l

3. $\frac{3}{4}$ litre = 0·_____ l = _____ ml

4. Medicine in a spoon is usually 50 ml ☐
   5 l ☐   5 ml ☐

5. $2\frac{1}{2}$ l = 2·_____ l = _____ ml

6. $\frac{1}{5}$ l = 0·_____ l = _____ ml

7. How many 500 ml in a 2 l bottle of water? _____

8. How many glasses each holding 100 ml can be filled from a $1\frac{1}{2}$ l bottle of orange? _____

9. $2\frac{1}{2}$ l plus 450 ml = _____

10. $1\frac{1}{4}$ l + 3·45 l + 6250 ml = _____

11. 200 ml of milk costs 35c. How much for 1 l? _____

12. I spilled 350 ml of water from a 1 l bottle. How much is left? _____

13. I drink 125 ml of apple juice each morning. How much do I drink in 1 week? _____

14. A bottle holds 120 ml of cough mixture. How many 5 ml spoons can be filled from the bottle? _____

15. Put in the correct sign: <, > or =.
    $\frac{1}{4}$ l _____ 200 ml

/15

Topic — Capacity. Problem solving. In your copy.

1. A 2 l bottle of orange costs €1·84.
   (a) How much would a litre cost? _____
   (b) How much would 500 ml cost? _____

2. How many glasses holding 200 ml could you fill from a 2 l bottle? _____

3. On a hot summer day Billy drank 86 ml of water, Adam drank 1·1 l and George drank 1 l 25 ml. How much water did they drink altogether? _____

4. Katie spilt 0·486 l from a 2 l bottle of blackcurrant, then filled her glass with 250 ml of blackcurrant. How much was left in the bottle? _____

5. If a bottle of cough medicine holds 75 ml and the doctor told you to take three 5 ml spoonfuls of medicine each day, how many days would the bottle of medicine last? _____

6. At Danielle's birthday party there are 15 guests. How many 2 l bottles of orange must Mum buy if each glass holds 180 ml? _____
   How much is left over in the last bottle? _____

7. 24 scouts go camping for two days. Each scout has a glass of orange juice in the morning in a glass that holds 200 ml.
   (a) How much orange juice will the scouts use on day 1? _____
   (b) How much orange juice will the scouts use altogether? _____
   (c) If the scoutmaster brought 10 l of orange juice, how much is left after breakfast on the second day? _____

/7

I. Mental Maths

Beat the clock.

Fill in the blanks.

1. $\frac{2}{3} + \underline{\quad} = 1$
2. $\frac{1}{8} + \underline{\quad} = 1$
3. $\frac{1}{6} + \underline{\quad} = 1$
4. $\frac{3}{5} + \underline{\quad} = 1$
5. $\frac{1}{2} + \underline{\quad} = 1$
6. $\frac{1}{4} + \underline{\quad} = 1$
7. $\frac{3}{9} + \underline{\quad} = 1$

8. $\frac{4}{10} + \underline{\quad} = 1$
9. $\frac{8}{12} + \underline{\quad} = 1$
10. $\frac{10}{10} + \underline{\quad} = 1$

Circle the larger fraction.

11. $\frac{1}{4}$ $\frac{3}{8}$
12. $\frac{2}{3}$ $\frac{5}{9}$
13. $\frac{3}{10}$ $\frac{4}{5}$

14. $\frac{1}{2}$ $\frac{8}{10}$
15. $\frac{1}{3}$ $\frac{1}{4}$
16. $\frac{16}{20}$ $\frac{2}{5}$
17. $\frac{2}{3}$ $\frac{1}{2}$
18. $\frac{2}{5}$ $\frac{1}{2}$
19. $\frac{3}{4}$ $\frac{7}{8}$
20. $\frac{3}{10}$ $\frac{3}{5}$

/20

J. Code Cracker

Each problem has a letter. Solve the problem and put the letter into the grid to reveal the message! You may use your calculator.

L $= (18{,}063 \div 9) - 1{,}437 = \underline{\quad}$

T $= (975 \div 5) \times 4 = \underline{\quad}$

P $= (2{,}158 - 1{,}694) \div 4 = \underline{\quad}$

N $= 60{\cdot}48 \div 8 = \underline{\quad}$

D $= 3{,}575 \div 5 = \underline{\quad}$

E $= (2{,}665 \div 13) \times 4 = \underline{\quad}$

S $= 9 + 5 + 16 + 5{\cdot}5 = \underline{\quad}$

I $= (2{,}480 \times 3) - 6{,}924 = \underline{\quad}$

G $= (635 \div 5) + (497 \div 7) = \underline{\quad}$

O $= \frac{4}{7}$ of $882 = \underline{\quad}$

570	820	780

35·5	570	820	820	116	516	7·56	198

715	504	198	35·5

570	516	820

K. Puzzle

Fill in the numbers 1 to 9. Each number is used only once. Each row is a maths equation. Each column is a maths equation. Remember BOMDAS!

	–		7	×		4	⁻25
+			–			÷	
		–				–	⁻5
×			+			–	
		+			+	1	14
51			⁻7			1	

A Table Time — Beat the clock.

1. (81 – 17) + 33 = ____
2. (41 + 49) x 2 = ____
3. (74 + 26) – 83 = ____
4. (85 – 15) ÷ 10 = ____
5. (96 ÷ 12) x 5 = ____
6. (18 x 3) + 17 = ____
7. (39 x 2) ÷ 6 = ____

8. (85 – 15) – 13 = ____
9. (37 + 42) + 24 = ____
10. (16 ÷ 4) x 10 = ____
11. (38 x 6) – 49 = ____
12. (70 + 80) ÷ 15 = ____
13. (49 – 16) x 4 = ____
14. (81 ÷ 9) + 13 = ____

15. (41 x 20) ÷ 10 = ____
16. (61 + 24) – 28 = ____
17. (43 x 3) + 47 = ____
18. (22 + 44) ÷ 6 = ____
19. (79 + 43) – 31 = ____
20. (46 – 13) x 3 = ____

/20

B Try this — Revise.

 Revision

Practice makes perfect!

1. Increase 250 by 20% ____
2. 74 x 18 = ____
3. Estimate 435 x 17. ____
4. Increase 110 by 25%. ____
5. Estimate 1026 + 379. ____

6. Decrease 530 by 35%. ____
7. 198 – 47. ____
8. Increase 450 by 10%. ____
9. 26 x 14 = ____
10. Decrease 600 by 80%. ____

/10

C Mental Maths — In your head.

1. 9 thirds of a cake makes ____ cakes.
2. The diameter of a circle is 11 cm. Find the radius. ____ cm
3. An octahedron has ____ faces.
4. 0·08 + 0·8 + 8 = ____
5. 90,006 – 8 = ____
6. Write 21:40 hours in 12 hour time. ____
7. Find the sum of 0·7 + 3·5. ____
8. 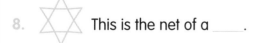 This is the net of a ____.
9. $\frac{7}{10} = \frac{}{100}$
10. 2 x 3 x 4 = ____
11. 7·25 – 3·9 = ____
12. How many edges on a square pyramid? ____

13. 5% of 80 = ____
14. What is the value of 1 in 36·821? tenths ☐ hundredths ☐ thousandths ☐
15. 9·37 x 3 = ____
16. 888 x 5 = ____
17. Siobhan shared 24 sweets between 6 children. How many sweets did each child get? ____
18. Does a nonagon or a decagon have 9 sides? ____
19. Write in ascending order. 0·90 0·19 9 0·09 _____
20. If lemonade costs 80c for 500 ml, how much will 3 l cost? ____

/20

D Vocabulary

Wordsearch.

1. There are _ _ _ _ _ _ months in winter.

2. The month before January is _ _ _ _ _ _ _ _.

3. How many 5c coins in 70c? _ _ _ _ _ _ _ _

4. A _ _ _ _ _ _ _ _ angle has 180°.

5. Four times twenty-one is _ _ _ _ _ _ –four.

6. Twenty-five times four = one _ _ _ _ _ _ _ _

7. How many threes in forty-eight? _ _ _ _ _ _ _

8. The first month of the year is _ _ _ _ _ _ _ _.

9. How many weeks in 3 fortnights? _ _ _

10. Eleven + seven + twelve = _ _ _ _ _ _

t	s	t	r	a	i	g	h	t	k
n	h	h	y	t	r	i	h	t	s
e	h	r	r	s	s	i	x	p	b
e	g	z	e	p	r	t	a	c	j
t	v	x	b	e	b	z	k	j	a
x	e	y	m	o	c	e	m	g	n
i	n	e	e	t	r	u	o	f	u
s	d	a	c	z	o	w	q	s	a
o	e	d	e	r	d	n	u	h	r
d	i	r	d	e	i	g	h	t	y

E Mental Maths

In your head.

1. 8 eighths of a cake is _____ cake.

2. $\frac{1}{2} > \frac{3}{4}$. True ☐ False ☐

3. $150 = 50 \times a$. $a =$ _____

4. [picture] Turn this picture 90° clockwise. _____

5. 9cm [box] x Area = 27cm². x = _____ cm

6. Find the perimeter of the shape in question 5. _____

7. ⁻6, ⁻4, ⁻2, _____, 2, 4

8. Is 8 nearer to 7·99 or 7·9? _____

9. Kevin ran around the 400m track 4 times. How far did he run altogether (in kilometres)? _____

10. Write $5\frac{2}{7}$ as an improper fraction. _____

11. $(35 \div 7) \times 8$. _____

12. Write the Roman numeral for 24. _____

13. How many 50c coins make up €10? _____

14. Write 15:15 hours in 12 hour time. _____

15. How many edges on a cube? _____

/15

F Puzzle

Problem of the week.

Sudoku

Fill in the boxes so the numbers 1 to 9 appear once in each row, column and small grid.

2		4	1					
			5		3	6		7
			9			4		
9			4				1	
6	5			1			7	4
	2				8			9
		9			5			
5		2	3		1			
			4	1		2		

G Topic

Number Sentences. In your head.

1. Put in the correct sign: +, -, x or ÷.

   81 ____ 9 = 9

2. 8 x ____ = 72

3. ____ − 39 = 75

4. Write fifty-six divided by seven equals two multiplied by four as an equation. ____

5. Put in the correct sign: <, > or =.

   72 − 18 ____ 8 x 8

6. Put in the correct sign: +, −, x or ÷.

   29 ____ 10 = 290

7. 16 + 15 > 30. True ☐ False ☐

8. 10 x 12 < 50 + 70. True ☐ False ☐

9. 93 − ____ = 52

10. 56 ÷ 7 = 12 − ____

11. ____ ÷ 9 = 14

12. $\frac{1}{2}$ of ____ = 15

13. 25% of ____ = 15

14. $\frac{3}{8}$ of 80 = ____

15. 80 − 26 > 7 x 9. True ☐ False ☐

  /15

H Topic

Number Sentences. Problem solving. In your copy.

1. Put in the correct sign: <, = or > .

   (a) 33 + 8 ____ 41   (b) 88 ÷ 11 ____ 2 x 4

   (c) 58 − 11 ____ 37   (d) 28 − 17 ____ 45 ÷ 5

   (e) 7 x 8 ____ 6 x 10   (f) 94 − 51 ____ 6 x 8

   (g) 33 + 44 ____ 7 x 10 (h) 34 + 17 ____ 3 x 20

2. Write these language sentences as mathematical sentences using +, x, =, < and >.

   (a) Nineteen is less than twenty-five. ____

   (b) Six plus seven is less than twenty. ____

   (c) Eight plus six is equal to fourteen. ____

   (d) Seventy-four is greater than eight times nine. ____

   (e) Fifty-six divided by eight equals thirteen minus six. ____

   (f) Fourteen minus seven is less than nine.

   ____

3. Write each of these as an equation. Then find the answer.

   (a) Andrew has seventy football cards. He gave his friend twenty and bought thirty-five more. How many has he now? ____

   (b) Having eaten twenty-five sweets Sheila still had thirty-two in the packet. How many had she at first? ____

   (c) How many bags with six pears in them could be filled from a box with eighty pears, and how many will be left over? ____

   (d) Teacher has thirty-three tests to correct. If she can correct six in an hour, how long will it take her to correct all the tests? ____

   (e) Brian had one hundred and fifty marbles. He kept sixty for himself and shared the rest equally among his six friends. How many did each get? ____

  /3

Mental Maths

Beat the clock.

What change will I get from €10 if I spend the following amounts?

1. €6·48 ____
2. €2·19 ____
3. €5·17 ____
4. €10·00 ____
5. €9·87 ____
6. €0·41 ____
7. €4·10 ____

8. €2·87 ____
9. €8·49 ____
10. €3·36 ____
11. €7·81 ____
12. €5·62 ____
13. €7·89 ____
14. €1·76 ____

15. €0·23 ____
16. €8·59 ____
17. €6·47 ____
18. €2·34 ____
19. €9·08 ____
20. €3·15 ____

/20

Code Cracker

Across

2. $\frac{1}{2}$ of (121 + 3689)
3. XXV
6. 10% of a millennium
7. 2000 ÷ 5
8. The smallest of 5,031, 3,510 and 5,103
10. (5,000 ÷ 2) – 25

Down

1. Five hundred thousand and sixty-three in figures
4. 7 x 8 x 9 x 10
5. 72,009 = ____ + 2000 + 9
9. (21 x 27) – 3

Puzzle

Karen has 4 times as many rings as Caoimhe. Karen and Caoimhe together have an even number of rings. They have more than 35 but less than 45. How many rings do they each have? ____

A Maths Facts | **General facts.**

Time

60 seconds = 1 minute
60 minutes = 1 hour
24 hours = 1 day
7 days = 1 week
14 days = 1 fortnight
52 weeks = 1 year
28–31 days = 1 month
365 days = 1 year
366 days = 1 leap year
10 years = 1 decade
100 years = 1 century
1000 years = 1 millennium

Dates

January = 31 days
February = 28 days (29 in a leap year)
March = 31 days
April = 30 days
May = 31 days
June = 30 days
July = 31 days
August = 31 days
September = 30 days
October = 31 days
November = 30 days
December = 31 days

Symbols

+	addition
–	subtraction
x	multiplication
÷	division
>	greater than
<	less than
=	equal to
≠	not equal to
°	degree
∠	angle
∟	right angle
⊥	is perpendicular to
=	parallel
%	per cent
·	decimal point
:	ratio

Length

mm = millimetre
cm = centimetre
m = metre
km = kilometre

Capacity

ml = millilitre
l = litre

Mass

g = gramme
kg = kilogramme

Signs

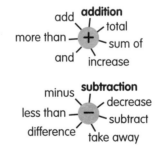

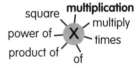

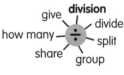

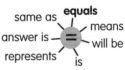

Parts of a calculator

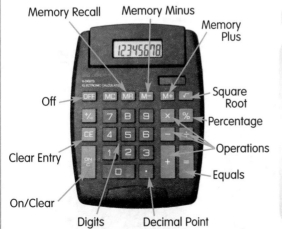

Memory Recall
Memory Minus
Memory Plus
Square Root
Off
Percentage
Clear Entry
Operations
On/Clear
Equals
Digits
Decimal Point

Roman numerals

I	V	X	L	C	D	M
1	5	10	50	100	500	1000

1. I
2. II
3. III
4. IV
5. V
6. VI
7. VII
8. VIII
9. IX
10. X
11. XI
12. XII
13. XIII
14. XIV
15. XV
16. XVI
17. XVII
18. XVIII
19. XIX
20. XX
21. XXI
22. XXII
23. XXIII
24. XXIV
25. XXV

Maths Facts

Fractions, decimals, percentages, rules and formulas.

Equivalent fractions

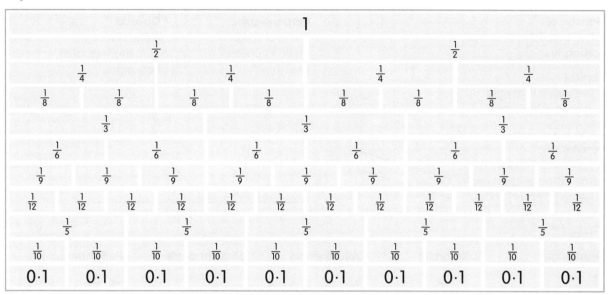

Fractions, decimals and percentages

Fraction	Decimals	Percentages
$\frac{1}{2}$	0·5	50%
$\frac{1}{4}$	0·25	25%
$\frac{3}{4}$	0·75	75%
$\frac{1}{8}$	0·125	$12\frac{1}{2}$%
$\frac{3}{8}$	0·375	$37\frac{1}{2}$%
$\frac{5}{8}$	0·625	$62\frac{1}{2}$%
$\frac{7}{8}$	0·875	$87\frac{1}{2}$%
$\frac{1}{3}$	0·333	$33\frac{1}{3}$%
$\frac{2}{3}$	0·666	$66\frac{2}{3}$%

Fraction	Decimals	Percentages
$\frac{1}{5}$	0·20	20%
$\frac{2}{5}$	0·40	40%
$\frac{3}{5}$	0·60	60%
$\frac{4}{5}$	0·80	80%
$\frac{1}{10}$	0·10	10%
$\frac{3}{10}$	0·30	30%
$\frac{7}{10}$	0·70	70%
$\frac{9}{10}$	0·90	90%
$\frac{1}{100}$	0·01	1%

Maths rules and formulas.

Rectangle
Perimeter
= 2 x (L + W)
Area = L x W

Square
Perimeter
= 4 x L
Area = L x W

L = length of shape
W = width of shape

SUM DETECTIVE – MATHS FACTS

Maths Facts — Lines, angles and 2D shapes.

Lines

Horizontal
A line parallel to the horizon.

Vertical
A line which is at right angles to a horizontal line.

Parallel
Lines that are always the same distance apart and have no common points.

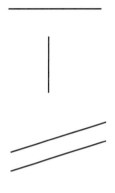

Perpendicular
A line at a right angle to another line.

Oblique
A line slanting from the vertical to horizontal.

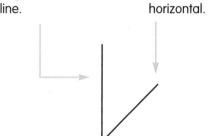

Angles

Right angle	Acute angle	Obtuse angle	Straight angle	Reflex angle

2D shapes. Triangles (3-sided figures).

Equilateral triangle
3 sides are the same length, and 3 angles the same size.

Isosceles triangle
2 sides the same length, and 2 angles the same size.

Right-angled triangle
One angle is 90°.

Scalene triangle
No sides are the same length, and no angles the same size.

 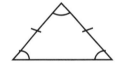 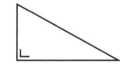 

2D shapes. Quadrilaterals.

Square
4 sides the same length. 4 angles the same size.

Rectangle
2 pairs of sides the same length. 4 angles the same size.

Rhombus
4 sides the same length. 2 pairs of angles the same size.

Parallelogram
2 pairs of sides the same length. 2 pairs of angles the same size.

Diamond
4 sides the same length. 4 angles the same size.

Trapezium
1 pair of sides the same length. 1 pair of sides different length. 2 pairs of angles the same size.

Other 2D shapes

Pentagon
5 sides
5 angles

Hexagon
6 sides
6 angles

Heptagon
7 sides
7 angles

Octagon
8 sides
8 angles

Decagon
10 sides
10 angles

Circle

Oval

      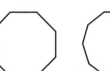

 **Maths Facts** 3D shapes.

3D shapes

Cube
6 faces
12 edges
8 vertices

Cuboid
6 faces
12 edges
8 vertices

Cylinder
3 faces
2 edges
0 vertices

Cone
2 faces
1 edge
1 vertex

Sphere
1 face
0 edges
0 vertices

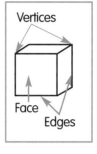

Triangular prism
5 faces
9 edges
6 vertices

Pentagonal prism
7 faces
15 edges
10 vertices

Hexagonal prism
8 faces
18 edges
12 vertices

Tetrahedron
(triangular based pyramid)
4 faces
6 edges
4 vertices

Square-based pyramid
5 faces
8 edges
5 vertices

Octahedron
8 faces
12 edges
6 vertices

Nets of 3D shapes

 Cube

 Tetrahedron (triangular based pyramid)

 Cuboid

Square-based pyramid

 Cylinder

Pentagonal prism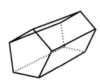

 Cone

Hexagonal prism

 Triangular prism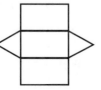

Octahedron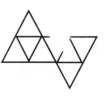

Abacus An instrument used for counting.

Acute An angle of less than 90 degrees.

Addition Putting two or more things together.

AM (Ante Meridian) The time between 12:00 (midnight) and 12:00 (midday).

Analogue clocks show time in analogue form.

Angle When two lines intersect, they make an angle:

– acute angle (<90°)

– right angle (90°)

– obtuse angle (>90°)

– reflex angle (>180°)

– straight angle (180°)

Anticlockwise Moving in the opposite direction to the hands of the clock.

Area The space taken up by a surface or 2D shape.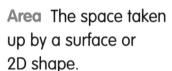

Ascending Arranging numbers from smallest to largest, e.g. 2, 3, 5, 9, 11.

Average Finding the total set of numbers and then dividing by the amount of numbers in the set.

Axis of symmetry An imaginary line through a shape. It divides the shape in two so that the sides will fold over exactly on top of each other.

Balance Used to show when two objects are equal in weight.

Bar graph Gives information using length of bars.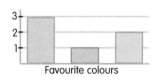

Base A line or face on which a shape is standing.

Block graph Gives information using blocks.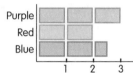

Calculator A device that works out sums quickly.

Calendar It shows us the days and months of the year.

Capacity A measure of how much something holds. 1000 millilitres in a litre.

Cent 100 cent in a euro.

Centimetre 100 centimetres in a metre.

Century 100 years in a century.

Chance How likely something is to happen.

Chord A line segment connecting 2 points on the arc of a circle.

Circle A 2D shape that has only one curved edge.

Circumference The distance (perimeter) around a circle.

Clockwise Moving in the same direction as the hands of the clock.

Column Numbers or words written vertically.

Composite number A number with more than 2 factors.

Cone A 3D shape that has a circular base and a point at the other end.

Consecutive Consecutive numbers follow in order without interruption, e.g. 14, 15, 16, 17.

Corner A point where two or more straight lines meet.

Cube A 3D shape with six equal square faces.

Cubit An old measurement of length from your elbow to the top of your middle finger.

Cuboid A 3D shape with six faces. Opposite faces are equal.

Currency The money used in a country, e.g. the euro.

Cylinder A 3D shape that has two circular ends and a curved surface joining the ends.

Data A collection of information.

Decagon A ten-sided 2D shape.

Decimal A number that has a decimal point. Used to show numbers that are not whole numbers, e.g. 48·23.

Deduct Another word for take away or subtract.

Definite Something that is certain to happen.

Denominator The number below the line in a fraction. $\frac{3}{4}$ ← denominator

Depth A measure of how deep something is, e.g. the swimming pool is 3 metres deep.

Descending Arranging numbers from largest to smallest, e.g. 17, 12, 6, 2.

Diagonal A straight line connecting two non-adjacent corners of a polygon.

Diagram A picture that is used to explain information.

Diameter A straight line connecting two points on the circumference of a circle and passing through the circle's centre.

Diamond A 2D shape that looks like a stretched square.

Difference The amount by which numbers are larger than or smaller than one another.

Digit Another name for a number.

Digital time Time that is shown without hands, e.g. **10:35**.

Dimension A dimension is a measure of size e.g. height, width, length.

Distance The length between two points.  Dublin 4 km

Division To share something into groups. These 9 balls are divided into 3 groups.

105

Divisor A number that goes into another number.

Double To make something twice as big or have twice as many.

Dozen An old term for 12 of something, e.g. a dozen eggs.

Edge The intersection of 2 faces of a 3D object.

Eighths When something is divided into 8 equal pieces, each piece is an $\frac{1}{8}$.

$\frac{1}{8}$

Equal Exactly the same value or size. 100 cm is equal to 1 m.

Equation A statement of equality between two expressions, e.g. 3 x 4 = 6 + 6.

Equilateral Having sides that are all equal in length, e.g. equilateral triangle.

Equivalent Fractions that have the same value are equivalent, e.g. $\frac{2}{8} = \frac{1}{4}$.

Euro The currency in Ireland and most of Europe. 100 cent = €1.

Estimate To make a guess using the information available.

Even chance A 50:50 chance that something will or will not happen.

Even numbers Numbers that can be divided by two.

Face The flat surface of a 3D object.

Factor A number which will divide evenly into another number.

Fortnight Two full weeks or 14 days.

Fraction A part of a group or of a whole number. $\frac{1}{3}$ is circled

Fraction wall A wall used to show equal fractions.

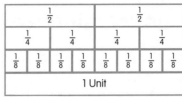

Frame The space left in a question for you to write, e.g. 4 + ____ = 10

Gramme A measurement used for weight. 1000 grammes in a kilogramme.

Graph A diagram that shows data. Also called a chart.

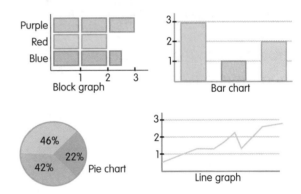

Block graph

Bar chart

46%
22%
42% Pie chart

Line graph

Grouping Sharing objects into groups that are equal in size.

Half When you divide something into two equal pieces, each one is called a half.

Handspan The distance between the tip of the thumb and the little finger on an outstretched hand.

Height Distance from top to bottom – how tall something is.

Hemisphere Half a sphere.

Heptagon A shape with 7 straight sides.

Hexagon A 2D shape that has 6 straight sides.

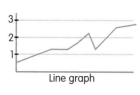

Highest common factor (HCF) The highest common factor that a given set of numbers has, e.g. HCF of 9 and 6 is 3.

Horizontal line A line or plane parallel to the horizon. _____

Hour A unit of time. 24 hours in a day. 60 minutes in an hour.

Hundredth When an object is divided into 100 pieces each one is a hundredth or $\frac{1}{100}$.

Impossible Something that will never happen.

Improper fraction A fraction whose numerator is equal to or greater than its denominator, e.g. $\frac{5}{2}$

Intersect When two lines cross over one another we say they intersect.

Irregular An irregular shape has sides and angles that are not equal to each other.

Isosceles An isosceles triangle has two equal sides and two equal angles.

Kilogramme A kilogramme is a measure of weight. 1000 grammes in a kilogramme.

Kilometre A kilometre is a measure for long distances. 1000 metres in a kilometre.

Kite A 4-sided 2D shape where opposite sides are equal.

Length The distance from one end of an object to the other end. Measured in centimetres, metres and kilometres.

Less than A symbol used to show that one number is less than another. (<). The narrow end points to the smaller number. 4 < 6.

Likely If something is likely, there is a good chance that it will happen.

Line graph A diagram using straight lines to join points representing certain information.

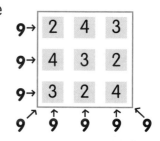
Line graph

Line of symmetry An imaginary line through a shape. It divides the shape in two so that the sides will fold over exactly on top of each other.

Liquid A fluid such as milk, which is measured using millilitres, litres and kilolitres.

Litre (l) A measure of capacity. There are 1000 millilitres in a litre.

Lowest common multiple (LCM) The lowest common multiple that a given set of numbers has, e.g. LCM of 9 and 6 is 18.

Magic square A square filled with numbers. The numbers in each row, column and diagonal all add up to the same amount.

9→	2	4	3
9→	4	3	2
9→	3	2	4

9 ↗ 9 ↑ 9 ↑ 9 ↑ 9 ↖

Measure To work out the size or amount of an object or distance.

Metre (m) A measure used for length or distance, e.g. 1 metre.

Millennium One thousand years.

Millilitre (ml) A measure used for small amounts of liquid.

Millimetre (mm) A measure used for small lengths.

Minus Another word for subtract, deduct or take away. 13 minus 7 is 6. 13 − 7 = 6.

Minute A measure of time. 60 seconds is one minute.

Minute hand The longer hand on a clock tells the minutes.

Minute hand

Mixed number A symbol representing a whole number and a fraction, e.g. $2\frac{4}{5}$.

Month A measure of time. There are 12 months in a year.

> 30 days has September,
> April, June and November.
> All the rest have 31.
> Except February alone,
> Which has 28 days clear
> And 29 in each leap year.

Multiple The product of two or more factors. 3, 6, 9, 12 are multiples of 3 because 3 is a factor of each.
The total of a number of groups or rows.

$5 \times 3 = 15$

Net A flat pattern that can be folded to make a 3D model of a shape.

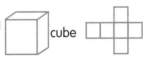
cube

Nonagon A nine-sided 2D shape.

Non-symmetrical Does not have symmetry/has no lines of symmetry.

Noon Midday. 12 o'clock in the day.

Number line A line used to show the position of a number.

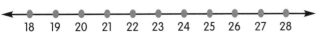
18 19 20 21 22 23 24 25 26 27 28

Number sentence A sentence written using numerals and symbols, e.g. 6 – 4 = 2.

Numerator Number above the line in a fraction. $\frac{3}{4}$ ← numerator

Oblique line A line slanting from the vertical to the horizontal.  oblique

Obtuse angle An angle greater than a right angle but smaller than a straight angle.

Octagon Any shape that has eight straight sides.

Odd number A number that cannot be divided evenly by two, e.g. 1, 3, 5, etc.

Operation One of the four methods of solving mathematical problems, e.g. addition, subtraction, multiplication or division.

Ordering Placing a group in order according to a given instruction, e.g. size, weight, length etc.

Ordinal number Tells position, e.g. 1st (first), 2nd (second), 3rd (third) etc.

Oval A closed curve that looks like a stretched circle.

Pair Two items together.

Parallel lines Two or more lines that will never meet and always remain the same distance apart, e.g. railway tracks.

Parallelogram A 2D shape with 4 sides. Opposite sides are parallel and the same length. Opposite angles are equal.

Pattern Numbers or objects that are arranged following a rule, e.g. 4, 7, 10. The rule is add 3.

Pentagon Any shape that has 5 straight sides.

Pentagonal prism
A prism with a pentagon at either end.

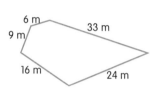

Percentage A quality expressed in hundredths (%).

Perimeter The distance around the outside of a shape. Add the lengths of all the sides.

6 m
9 m
33 m
16 m
24 m

Perpendicular lines make right angles when they meet.

Pictogram Uses pictures to show data. A key is used to interpret the pictures.

Sandwiches eaten at a party

Ham
Tomato
Cheese
Peanut butter
Jam

Key:
= 5 sandwiches

Pie chart Uses a circle to show data. Sections of the circle are used to represent data.

Children
Men
Women
60 people attending a circus

Place value Value according to place in a number, e.g. 963. The place value of 6 is 60.

Plus Another word for add. 6 plus 9 is the same as 6 + 9.

PM (Post Meridian) The time from midday to midnight.

Polygon A 2D shape with three or more straight sides.

Prime number A number with only 2 factors, itself and 1.

Prism A 3D object. It has two identical ends. All its other faces are rectangles.

These 3D shapes are all prisms.

Product When two or more numbers are multiplied the answer is the product, e.g. 6 x 3 = 18.

Pyramid A 3D object. It has one base. All its other faces are triangles.

A Pentagonal pyramid   B Square pyramid   C Hexagonal pyramid   D Triangular pyramid

Quarter One of four equal parts of a group or object. Written as $\frac{1}{4}$.

$\frac{1}{4}$ of the rectangle $\frac{1}{4}$ of the stars

Radius A line joining the centre of a circle to a point on the circle's circumference.

radius

Ratio The relationship between two numbers, e.g. 2 is to 10 = 1:5.

Rectangular numbers A number whose units can be arranged into a rectangle, e.g. 20.

Regular polygon A polygon that has all sides equal in length and all angles are equal. The opposite is irregular.

Regular shape A shape that has all sides equal in length and all angles equal.

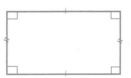

Rectangle All angles are right angles. Opposite sides are equal.

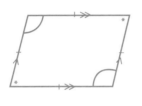

Remainder The amount left over when one number cannot be divided evenly by another e.g. $13 \div 4 = 3$ with 1 left over. 1 is the remainder.

Rhombus A 2D shape with 4 sides. All sides are the same length. Opposite sides are parallel. Opposite angles are equal.

Right angle An angle that measures 90°. These angles are all right angles.

Roman numeral Letters that represent numbers used by ancient Romans, e.g. v = 5, vi = 6.

Rotation A turn in a clockwise or anticlockwise direction.

Round/rounding off An approximate answer, e.g. round 69 to the nearest 10: 70. Round 548 to the nearest 100: 500.

Scalene triangle A triangle that has sides of different lengths. The angles are different sizes.

Scales Instrument used to weigh objects.

Season 4 seasons in a year: spring (3 months); summer (3 months); autumn (3 months); winter (3 months).

> Spring: February, March, April.
> Summer: May, June, July.
> Autumn: August, September, October.
> Winter: November, December, January.

Second A very short measure of time. 60 seconds equals 1 minute.

Semicircle Half a circle.

Sequence A list of numbers, letters or objects which are in a special order, e.g. 1, 2, 3, 4, 5.

Set A collection of objects or numbers. Each member is an element of the set.

Set square An instrument shaped like a right-angled triangle. It can be used to draw right angles, perpendicular and parallel lines.

Sharing Dividing into equal groups or parts.

Simplify To change into simpler terms, e.g. $\frac{25}{30} = \frac{5}{6}$.

Skip counting Counting on or counting back in groups of the same size, e.g. 2, 4, 6, 8.

Sphere A 3D shape shaped like a ball.

Square A 2D shape with four equal sides and four right angles.

110

Square number A number whose units can be arranged into a square, e.g. 4.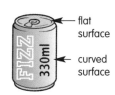

Straight line The shortest distance between two points.

Strategy A method for working something out, e.g. 73 x 10 = 730. A good strategy for multiplying by 10 is to add a zero.

Subtraction Take one number away from another, e.g. 23 – 9 = 14.

Sum The total when numbers are added. 4 + 6 = 10. 10 is the sum of 4 and 6.

Surface The top or outside layer of an object. It can be flat or curved.

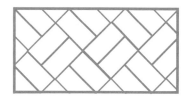

flat surface

curved surface

Surface area The total area of all the surfaces of a 3D object.

Symbol A sign or letter used instead of words. + (plus), = (equals).

Symmetry/symmetrical
When one half of a shape is a mirror image of the other half. When folded on an axis of symmetry one half fits exactly on top of the other.

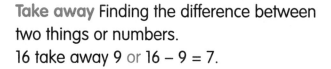

Take away Finding the difference between two things or numbers.
16 take away 9 or 16 – 9 = 7.

Tally marks Marks used to help when counting a large number. They are drawn in bundles of 5. = **18**

Tetrahedron A polyhedron with four faces, e.g. triangular pyramid.

Tessellation A pattern made of identical shapes. The shapes fit together without any gaps. The shapes do not overlap.

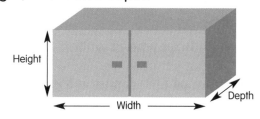

Three-dimensional (3D) An object that has height, width and depth.

Height

Width

Depth

Time The space between one event and the next. The space taken by an action. It takes 1 minute for my heart to beat 80 times.

Times Another word for multiply. 4 times 7 is the same as 4 x 7.

Timetable A table where times are organised for when things happen, e.g. school timetables, train timetables and TV timetables.

TV TIMETABLE
3:00   Kids TV
3:20   Cartoons
3:45   Kits Pet Vet
4:00   Son of Tarzan

Total Add all the numbers to find the total. 13 + 9 + 31 = 53. 53 is the total.

Trapezium A quadrilateral plane figure in which only one pair of opposite sides are parallel.

Triangle A shape with three straight sides.

Triangular prism A 3D shape. It has two identical ends which are triangles. All its other faces are rectangles.

Twelve hour time Time is told in twelve hour sections e.g. 12 midnight to 12 noon is a.m. time. 12 noon to 12 midnight is p.m. time.

Twenty-four hour time Time is told in twenty-four hour sections (1 day = 24 hours). 4 digits are used e.g. 8:30 am in 24 hour time is written as 08:30.
5:45 pm in 24 hour time is written as 17:45.

Two-dimensional (2D) A shape that has only two dimensions: length and width.

Unequal Not equal to (≠). 6 + 8 ≠ 7 + 9.

Unit A unit is one.

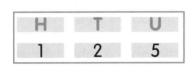

H	T	U
1	2	5

1 hundred   2 tens   5 units

Value The worth given to something, e.g. ● the value of this coin is 5 cent.

12 + ____ = 19. The value of ____ is 7.

Vertex (vertices) The point where two or more straight lines meet.

Vertex

Vertical line A line which is at right angles to a horizontal line.

Telegraph poles are vertical.

Volume The amount of space taken up by an object.

Week A time period of seven days. Monday, Tuesday, Wednesday, Thursday, Friday, Saturday, Sunday.

Weight The heaviness of an object. This bag of sugar weighs 2 kg.

Width How wide an object is. Your finger is about 1 centimetre wide.

Year A time period of 12 months. Starts on 1st January and ends on 31st December.
365 days in a normal year and 366 days in a leap year.

Zero Has no value. Also called nought. Written as 0.